Exploring Twin Relationships
Is Being a Twin *Always* Fun?

Exploring Twin
Relationships
Is Being a Twin
Always Fun?

Betty Jean Case

Tibbutt Publishing
Portland, Oregon

Library of Congress Cataloging in Publication Data
Case, Betty Jean
    Exploring Twin Relationships: Is Being A Twin Always
Fun?/Betty Jean Case. – Portland, OR: Tibbutt Pub. Co., ©
1996.
    p. , cm.

    ISBN: 0-9629948-2-0

1. Twins–Psychology. 2. Twins–Family relationships.
I. Title.

BF723.T9

                                        155.4'44 dc20
            Library of Congress Catalog Number 96-90382

            Tibbutt Publishing Company, Inc.
            0438 S.W. Palatine Hill Road
            Portland, Oregon 97219

About the Author

Betty Jean Case grew up in a totally twin environment with a twin sister and twin brothers. It was the birth of twin grandsons that caused her to reflect back upon her life lived as a twin. "To what degree has my life been influenced because of twinship?" she pondered.

Anxious to learn more about twins, she researched over 800 identical and fraternal twins worldwide, most between the ages of twenty and seventy. Not only was she startled by her findings, she was also able to gain greater insight into her own relationship between herself and her twin.

In her first book, *We Are Twins, But Who Am I?*, she lets twins tell about how they felt about being a twin as they grew up; their feelings of security as well as insecurity. They expressed gratitude for being given the opportunity to tell—many of them for the first time—how their emotions went from happiness to despair as they saw their performance being compared with their twin.

Her second book, *Living Without Your Twin*, was written after she recognized there was little information available to help twins who had lost their twin, whether due to death or estrangement. The author has since lost one of her twin brothers through death.

In this, her third book, she has taken five sets of twins from each of the five categories of twins and looked in greater depth into what made being a twin a happy or not so happy experience. She has also included chapters dealing specifically with twins and their relationships with siblings, parents, spouse, and grandparents, and their relationships with family members after loss of their twin.

Betty Jean welcomes your comments and questions. You may contact her by writing:

Betty Jean Case
Tibbutt Publishing
0438 SW Palatine Hill Road
Portland, Oregon 97219
Telephone (503) 246-6748

Acknowledgments

It would be impossible for me to recognize in print all of the people who have directly or indirectly played a part in making this book a reality. I have been overwhelmed by the willingness of twins to share their personal twin experience with me. I am also indebted to the many parents of twins, siblings, and friends of twins who have contributed to this book.

I am most grateful to numerous mothers of twins groups throughout the world who have given me the opportunity to meet and speak with their members. All of you know who you are.

My sincere thanks to the radio and television stations both in the United States and abroad who have let me share my enthusiasm and knowledge about twins with their listeners. My appreciation to the newspaper media who have given space in their papers to let me talk about twins.

To the twin sets in this book who have given their permission to use their stories, and the liberty to change their names, I want to say "Thank you." The book would never have been written without you. By your sharing of yourself, others will benefit.

My heartfelt gratitude goes to you, Terri Walker, who worked diligently with me on the book, both in editing and preparing it for the printer. You were ever patient, cooperative, and understanding. Thanks to you, Terri, the book is born.

This book is lovingly dedicated to my parents, Leda Fay and John Perry Tibbutt, who launched not one, but two sets of twins; also to my understanding and supportive husband, Laurel, and my twin sister, Fay Louise, who made me a twin.

Contents

Preface

"I *always* thought it would be fun to be a twin," is a comment that has often been made by those who are not a twin. I said, "It should be, but it isn't *always*. Why?"

Twenty-five sets of twins, both identical and fraternal, tell you what their life has been like as a twin. The reader will be able to see what made their lives with a built-in playmate a wonderful experience or a regrettable one.

It's a book about relationships. The reader will become aware of the influence each twin has upon the other. The book will guide parents of twins in a direction that will help them make twinship memorable for their children. Non-twins will learn how to interact with twins in a positive instead of a negative way.

Foreword

The fascination with twins lies far back in time. Indeed, there has never been an era that was immune to the mysteries surrounding them. That is only part of the story, however, since various cultures have treated multiples differently. From the American Indians who generally revered twins, to certain African tribes who killed twin infants and their mother, to Asian cultures in which the birth of twins was simply left unrecorded so their existence was a moot point, to the merely curious attitudes of today's cultures, twins have gained the spotlight simply because there were two of them. But what were their lives like? How did they feel about this unusual relationship?

In earlier volumes Ms. Case has examined the feelings a fraternal twin has when she is attempting to define her own identity (*We Are Twins, But Who Am I?*), and the excruciating sense of loss a twin experiences when he or she loses their lifelong partner (*Living Without Your Twin*). In this new volume, *Exploring Twin Relationships: Is Being a Twin Always Fun?* she offers the insights of twins about their twin relationship. While some feel very positive about their condition, others have found only trouble and confusion around their twinship. This book adds to the increasing body of knowledge about human multiples that has been developing in recent years. It reflects the fact that we are living in a time of increasing births of multiples. The birth of twins has risen 33 percent between 1978 and 1988 and the births of triplets and higher order births has exploded by 131 percent in that same time period. Naturally, there has been increasing publicity about these children. And with the attention comes additional complications in their lives as well as the lives of those rearing them.

Twins, themselves—whether they are identical, same-sex fraternal or opposite-sex fraternal—all have contributed their personal views of the pros and cons of growing up a twosome. "I left home at eighteen to move to another state to escape competitiveness, to be on my own," says a fraternal male. "Despite everyone making an issue of it, I never felt like a twin. I have often thought about my twinship, but of all my five brothers and sister, I am least close to my twin." Such a negative response is balanced, however, by another who writes that he and his brother keep in touch quite often although they live a distance from each other. The yin and yang of the twin relationship is prominent in these stories.

Female fraternal twins are a somewhat different matter, according to Ms. Case's findings. There seems to be more positive attitudes expressed by them about their twin and the relationship they have enjoyed together. Although one pair wrote, "The negative aspect of being a twin for us was that we fought an awful lot." According to another pair, "Play was a big part of my childhood and an important step towards my development. It began in the backyard where I first began to stand up for my twin. I learned that it proved helpful when we both worked at a project together. We learned through play that one of us might excel in one activity and not in another. We learned how to reassure one another and help build self-confidence."

The author offers advice to parents on rearing the separate kinds of twins based on her own experience (she is a fraternal same-sex twin and has twin grandchildren) and on the examination of these comments from twins themselves. She looks into the special relationships with twins and other siblings, with parents, with grandparents, and with spouses. Since the arrival of a pair of twins in a family can be either a magnificent challenge or a problem if there are other siblings, especially an only child, this advice can prove helpful to parents of twins. If twins appear to the uninitiated as islands unto themselves, they know themselves to be connected by complex strata of shared sympathies, insights and destinies. Consciously and unconsciously they are part of a larger order of things that they can only partially comprehend. What they do understand, however, they are often willing to share with those not born with a partner. In this new volume, Ms. Case has captured some of that willingness of twins to help others as well as themselves.

Kay Cassill

Kay Cassill is the author of Twins: Nature's Amazing Mystery, *a comprehensive volume on the mysteries surrounding twins and other multiples. She is the Founding President of The Twins Foundation, a fourteen-year-old non-profit organization which is the country's primary research information center on twins. It serves twins, their families, the media, medical and social scientists and the general public through its publications, its National Twin Registry and its multi-media resource center.*

John Perry Tibbutt (Father), standing. Left to right: Fay Louise, Leda Fay Tibbutt (Mother), Betty Jean. Front, left to right: Torrence Ness (Tod) and Theodore Van (Ted).

Introduction

I've had the privilege of talking with hundreds of parents of twins and have found their greatest desire is for their twin children to be friends as adults. In all families with more than one child, there will be friction between siblings. We would worry if this were not so; something would be wrong.

It is always sad when the bond between twins that was formed at the time of conception somehow becomes fractured. The reasons for this are many, and often complex.

Fourteen years have passed since I first began to gather research material on twins. This time lapse will be a real advantage to me now as I tap, once again, into the lives of some of these twins and find out how, or if, their relationship with their twin has improved, or deteriorated.

My research files contain over 800 questionnaires answered by identical and fraternal twins, from all walks of life. Near the end of the book you will find the questionnaire each of these twins completed, independently of one another.

I have chosen to include both identical and fraternal twins. All twins share much in common, yet there are indeed issues that face identical twins that are not a problem for fraternal twins, and vice versa. As you read these case histories you will gradually see the strong influence that genetics seems to play in the unfolding lives of identical twins.

Until recent years the fraternal twins have been somewhat ignored from a psychological standpoint. I've cringed when the remark has been made to me that, "I've never thought that

fraternal twins are really twins, but more like siblings in a family."
Of course this is true genetically, but the fact that these fraternal
twins are born and enter the world as a "pair" places them in a
different situation that the lone child who enters the arms of a
family who have all eyes on one child, not two.

Opposite sex twins have been especially neglected. I well
remember the comment of one mother after I spoke to a Mothers
of Twins group, I believe in Australia. She said, "Somehow we've
become lost in the shuffle."

I have chosen to include five sets of twins from each of the
five categories of twins. The selection has not been easy. Many
of these twins have bared their souls to me, sharing their personal
thoughts about how they view their twinness and their relationship
with their twin. Their ages vary from sixteen to into the eighties,
with the majority of them being between twenty and seventy
years old. The names of the twins in this book have been changed,
unless the twins requested that their real names be used. All have
been willing to let their stories be used in hopes that this may, in
some way, help parents spare their twin children any pain they
may have experienced in childhood.

As you familiarize yourself with these fifty twins, try as best
you can, to walk in their shoes. While none of them would trade
away their twinship for singleton status, for some of them,
twinship has complicated their lives to the point that they have
sought psychological counseling.

Before reading their individual stories, note the size of their
family, whether there were other siblings and, if so, whether they
were older or younger. When there is just one set of twins and no
siblings there is usually a much greater likelihood that all eyes
will be focused on twinship.

What these twins have to say may help parents of twins avoid
a lot of headaches and heartaches. Those twins who were not
threatened by competition, comparison, expectations, and
favoritism, and who felt in tune with their twin, have loved being
a twin. The twins who reflect back and recall how they felt when
they were being compared, etc., hasten to reinforce their belief
that twins should have been recognized for who they were, first

as an individual, then a twin. Resentment often surfaced when they were seen as one instead of being two separate selves. There is always the exception: a few twins want to be seen as 'one.'

In order for you to get the total picture of these twin sets, it is important that you view their growth from infancy through adulthood. In the viewing, hopefully you can recognize what might have caused the healthy or unhealthy relationships that exists in these twins' lives. The greater part of our lives is spent as an adult, but what went on in our childhood years is vitally important. Twins may agonize more than single siblings do if they do not feel close as adults. Twins are just supposed to feel closer to one another.

As you read, observe what it was in their childhood that appeared to put them in conflict with one another. Or, on the positive side, what was it that made them feel close and comfortable with one another. Clues about their feelings will be evident in their open-ended comments after their responses to questions asked about their childhood.

When you read about their relationship with parents, try to glean from them what it was in the relationship that could have caused friction or conversely, what was it that made them comfortable with their parents and with their twin. Try to see if you can assess what it was that caused them to feel as they do about themselves as adults and their relationship with their twin.

It is my hope and prayer that you will see twins as individuals who want to be known and treated as individual people, not clones of one another. In fairness to one set of twins who will be a part of this book, I qualify the previous statement.. This pair of twins tells me that they want only to be identified with one another, not separately. I honor their wish, as I do all the other twin participants.

Chapter One

A Look Into the
Lives of Identical Twins

"We were groomed to look *exactly* alike. One time one of us lost a front tooth. Mother wiggled the 'twin' tooth until it also came out."

Of all the twins, it is this group that often wants, and tolerates, the look-alike scene.

Genetically, identical twins are as alike as two human beings can possibly be. Barring mutations in development, twins who result from the splitting of a single ovum fertilized by a single sperm are truly identical in their genetic makeup. Thus, any differences between them can only result from environment and experience. This fact has made identical twins very interesting to researchers who study the relative impact on human development of "heredity vs environment," or "nature vs nurture." Studies of identical twins who were separated at birth have revealed fascinating data about just how much of human behavior is indeed caused by genetic makeup, rather than by individual experience or choice.

Statistics show that identical twins make up about one third of the twin population. Of these, approximately one fourth are what have been labeled as mirror-image twins. With mirror-image twins one of them will be left handed. If one has a mole on the right side of the forehead, there will be one on the left side of the other twin. The whorl of the hair will go in opposite directions with these twins.

One of the exciting experiences I've known in doing twin research is the exhilaration I've felt when I've been able to help twins learn if they are identical. Some have been surprised to find out they are not only identical but mirror-image as well.

While it is the interest of many twin researchers to learn and study the genetics of twins, my interest has been in the psychological makeup of twins. What impact does being a twin have upon a person's life?

Do I love my twin? Of course I do. Then how can I love her and hate her at the same time?

Before we examine the many types of twin relationships that exist between identicals, this must be said.

1. Of all the hundreds of twins I have researched, the love bond that appears to exist between identical twins is the most intense I've ever known.

2. These twins who are genetically the same often feel they are "one" instead of two. Some of these twins are happiest when they are with their twin, and because of that, choose to live their entire lives together.

3. Many of these twins cannot bear to think of living life apart from their twin; hence when they lose their twin to death it is as though a part of them is gone.

Knowing the facts stated above, it is tragic when forces within their lives fracture the joy of being an identical twin. It is for this reason we will be delving into the lives of various sets of identical twins to find out what it was in their developmental years that resulted in the unhappiness of the twins.

Whether we like to believe it or not, all of us really like to be thought of as unique. Most of us don't have this as a problem, but twins know well what it is like to be confused with another. Confusion may be caused by having another who looks much like themselves, or because of having a name very similar to theirs, or simply because they are a twin.

Twinship, a Gift Money Cannot Buy

Even if they could, the large majority of these twins would not trade away their twinship for a life as a singleton. The problems encountered due to twinship are far outweighed by the joys and satisfactions they have known due to having someone who knows them better than anyone else.

Identical twins have many more positive feelings about their twinship than negative.

Identical twins find the questions so often put to them boring. They are repeatedly asked, "What's it like being a twin? Which one's the oldest?" The question that many of them find the most frustrating is this one, "Can you tell each other apart?" As one twin wrote, "We have always thought those questions were not very well thought out before spoken. But they are funny from a twin's point of view."

Most identical twins, even as adults, find themselves thinking in terms of "we" instead of "I." Writes this twin in his early 40s, "I still tend to think of myself as 'We' rather than 'I.' It's marvelous to have a sympathetic in life. I've always seen my twin as the 'senior partner.' He was born first, and entered the ministry six weeks before I did."

These twins want to be known as individuals, yet they understand that to have another who looks so much like them, may make it more difficult to be perceived as totally individual. "Just because we may look very much alike does not mean we think and act alike," was the comment of many of these twins.

Some of the twins told me that as children they used to be paraded before people who wanted to see the twins. Human nature being what it is, some of these twins enjoyed the limelight that was given them because of their being twins. Many of them did not like being stared at as people compared their alikeness.

Some identical twins are delighted when they find people cannot find differences in them, but they are the exceptions. Most identicals appreciate people being aware of the uniqueness of each twin.

Yet, some of these twins have capitalized on their looking alike. One set of twins is a prime example of this. These male twins readily admit they chose to be a part of the Ringling Brothers circus because they like to perform and be in front of an audience.

These twins understand the natural curiosity of people and are somewhat forgiving to the non-twin who will compare them. Yet they would like people to know they do not like being compared with their twin. They would rather be seen for who they are, each a unique person. As one twin wrote, "I think people need to understand that most twins do not like being compared. Even though we may look alike and have the same body chemistry, our personalities are very different. People can get to know twins individually and they will find this to be true. My friends have. Also 'the Bobsey twins' or 'the Bailly twins' are not terms that are cute or heartwarming. It can be embarrassing because people haven't tried to get to know us as people."

Some identical twins feel fraternal twins are not in quite the same league with them. It is true that identical twins are in a very real way quite different from the fraternal in that they are genetically the same.

There's a little song that goes like this, and it is a most fitting way to describe the feelings of a vast majority of these twins. Perhaps you will remember singing this song as a child.

"The more we get together, together, together,
The more we get together, the happier we'll be,
For your friends are my friends,
And my friends are your friends,
The more we get together, the happier we'll be."

This could well be the thoughts of many identical twins.

One identical twin, Sally Rempe chose to express her feelings about twinship in this poem.

"I looked at myself
Hazel eyes, blond hair to my shoulders.
I felt strange.
I said, 'Good morning'
This mirror image of myself
Replied greeting back to me.
I felt weird.
My shadow followed me around through the day
I picked up my pencil and took a side view
She gave me her smile,
I returned it.
I tripped on the way home
And cut my leg.
She cried along with me.
She felt it.
I slipped into bed
I turned over.
I felt happy
I looked at myself in her.
I didn't feel strange.
She was sleeping
I was awake.
We were looking through a looking glass
But one which had two sides."

One year this set of twins decided, without any previous
knowledge from the other that they wanted to honor their twin's
birthday with a personal touch. One twin wrote a song for her
twin, the other a poem. The poem Edith wrote for her twin
Elizabeth follows.

For Elizabeth

by Edith Maxey

I have this very special friend
I've known for many years.
Together we've shared everything
Good times, laughter, and tears.

This special friend won't turn away
When troubles I must bear.
She lends an ear and listens
In a way that shows she cares.

The happiest moments ever spent
Are in her company
When my mood is at its darkest,
She'll set my worries free.

Life's riches may have passed me by,
But still, I have a treasure
For in our golden friendship
I've found wealth beyond all measure.

My love for her goes very deep;
The secret lies herein-
This special girl who's my best friend
Is also my loving TWIN.

Though we are many miles apart,
Our love will know no death.
This poem is for my joy of life—
For you, Elizabeth.

The next poem was written by Karen Mills. Karen writes, "Last year Sharon and I lived 80 miles apart. I wrote this poem at a time when I was especially lonely for her."

"I feel empty and alone.
I have not my best friend close by,
Nor my unconditional supporter.
The one who knows my thoughts,
And feels my pain,
And listens, is not here.

For the first time in my life,
I am alone.
But somehow, I feel strong.
Like I can do anything.
I can live without her 'my twin.'
Because she is not far.
For she is a part of me."

I find the humor of some of these identical twins to be exhilarating. They are fun to be around. Some of the scenarios I've heard over the years give you a sense of their close resemblance to one another.

Here is the comical scene told to me by a very look-alike identical.

"One day I was sewing and needed thread. I went to Newberry's, the dime store, and picked out the thread, and took it over to the cashier to pay for it. The clerk asked me where the material was. I told her I was just buying a spool of thread. 'But where is the material,' she asked. I told her again I was just buying a spool of thread. 'But what about the material?' the clerk asked. Just then my twin sister stepped up to the counter with material. The poor cashier just put her head in her hands and bent down on the counter. I did not know my twin was in the store. We were both wearing a coat and hat that were alike. So, I got away by paying for just my spool of thread. (This same cashier had measured the material for my twin, who was just looking around in the store. My twin had not known that I had come in until she came to the cashier to pay for her material.)

"Another time I was visiting my twin sister in the hospital. As I was leaving, the nurse took me by the arm and asked where I was going. I told her I was going home. The nurse replied, 'You can't go home as the doctor wants to do more tests.' I told the nurse it didn't matter, I was going home. Then I led her back to my sister's room and pointed to her bed. Then I asked the nurse, 'May I go home now?'"

Do twins have ESP? This is a question I am often asked. My usual reply is that I have no scientific evidence that would prove twins are especially gifted in this area. I must say enough of my twin respondents have told of unusual coincidences that make me wonder if these occurrences are not known by twins more than the non-twin. What part does genetics play in this equation? I don't know, but it would seem plausible that since these twins are identical, their actions, feelings and thoughts might parallel in some way. I am more inclined to believe the closeness these twins know as little ones growing up may have more to do with this than the genetic aspect. There is still much we have to learn in this area.

The following comment made by one of these identical twins is an example of what I've had told me so very often in letters from twins.

"One time my twin came down to spend the summer with me. She said, 'I can't wait to show you a dress I just bought.' When she showed it to me I told her I had bought one just like it."

I often enter a room and find my sister singing the same song that I have going through my head.

This letter is from an identical twin; however, she writes it with all twins in mind. "After attending twin conventions, I feel I would like to have more twins find the normal sharing feelings, but not the abnormalities our society focuses on. I feel we're special people, unique individuals, but not that it caused a burden or identity crisis... I hate to hear some of the sick stories about twins sharing the same brain, death trauma, etc. Some of those people would probably have had the same abnormal personalities if they had been born a singleton, but because of their being twins it gets attributed to twinship."

A small minority have found being an identical twin has been the greatest gift life could offer. They would make few changes, if any, in their life due to twinship. A few of them have gone into a profession where they would continue to be in the limelight, such as acting, or social service work.

The majority of these twins feel twinship has placed them in a special and privileged group. Very early in life they have become aware of people being drawn to them due to their being two who look almost, if not totally, alike.

Some of these twins have purposely chosen to enter into a different type of work in order to eliminate competition with their twin, while others have, after much soul searching, decided it is alright to enter into the same type of work.

An excellent example of this is the Twin's Restaurant, an eclectic downtown restaurant on the upper eastside of Manhattan in New York City.

Lisa and Deborah Ganz, identical twins, along with actor Tom Beringer, are owners of this unique restaurant. Their staff consists of thirty-seven sets of twins, all identical. The close bond these women share is evident as they continue to do what they enjoy doing—being together and serving up great meals.

Most identicals want to feel they have a close bond with their twin, and those who do not express guilt over not feeling as close to their twin as they would like. By studying over the entire questionnaire of each set of twins and evaluating their responses, it was possible to discover what it was in their relationship that caused less than comfortable feelings in each of them. "I wish," was often used in the responses of these twins. "I wish my father had not shown favoritism for my twin." "I wish I had not allowed my twin to dominate me when we were growing up." "I wish our parents had let us be more individual instead of our always having to go everywhere together." "I wish I had learned early in life to stand on my own two feet rather than be content to remain in the shadow of my twin."

Most, if not all of these twins, expressed deep love for their twin, even though some felt it is good that they do not live near one another. Yet, there are some twins who only find complete happiness when they can see or talk to their twin every day.

The majority of these twins wish they had not been dressed alike as long as they were. They feel it delayed their recognition of each other as individuals. Yet, there are a few who have enjoyed dressing alike all their lives.

Most identical have strong feelings about their relationship with their twin. They feel, and rightly so, that they are the only ones able to know how they truly feel about their twin, and the degree of closeness they want to maintain. If the relationship is equally fulfilling to each of them, and they find happiness in their relationship, then it must be right for them.

I close this chapter with a poem about identical twins. It brings a roar of laughter whenever I tell it.

The Twins
by Gurney Williams

In form and feature, face and limb,
I grew so like my brother,
That folks got taking me for him,
And each for one another.
It puzzled all our kith and kin,
It reached a fearful pitch;
For one of us was born a twin,
Yet not a soul knew which.

One day, to make the matter worse,
Before our names were fixed,
As we were being bathed by nurse,
We got completely mixed;
And thus you see, by fate's decree,
OR rather nurse's whim;
My brother John got christened me,
And I got christened him.

This fatal likeness even dogged
My footsteps when at school
And I was always getting flogged,
For John turned out a fool.
I put this question, fruitlessly
To everyone I know,
"What would you do, if you were me,
To prove that you were you?"

Our close resemblance turned the tide
Of my domestic life,
For somehow, my intended bride
Became my brothers' wife.
In fact, year after year the same
Absurd mistakes went on,
And when I died, the neighbors came
And buried brother John.

Chapter Two

Identical Men

Jerry and Don

These twins had an older and a younger brother.

I chose these men because of the powerful influence twinship has had upon their marriages.

Childhood

The responses to their childhood questions were almost identical, but not quite. Jerry considered himself the leader. Don, his twin brother, felt competitive with his twin.

These men looked very much alike and were often mistaken for one another. They did not feel inferior to each other, and neither was jealous of the other. They were in the same classroom until they went to college.

Here is what they said about competition in their childhood. Jerry commented, "We did compete academically in grade and high school, but the competition was not acute."

Don wrote, "As a child I just accepted it, because that was the way it always had been. As an adult it was the source of considerable humor."

They had this to say in response to the question, "What stands out as being positive or negative as a child regarding twinship? Jerry said, "I have always enjoyed being a twin. I still enjoy it. I felt as a child that being a twin was unusual and special." Don wrote, "I do not think other people realize the degree of kinship and closeness that most twins feel. (I am speaking of identical twins.) We fought each others' wars and shared each others' laughter. If there was anything negative about our twinship, it came from outside forces."

One of these men shared this regarding competition, "My twin and I grew up competing with one another. We have always continued that attitude in business and have both achieved modest success because of it."

Parent/Child Relationship

Don felt favoritism was shown him by his mother, and Jerry commented that he felt that favoritism was shown his brother. Don felt his parents compared their performance—Jerry did not. Both felt they were encouraged to participate in their choice of extra-curricular activities.

When asked to share anything they would like about their relationship with their parents, Jerry said, "Our father was a very objective, consistant man. When it is all over I would hope to have the same feeling and respect from my sons that I feel toward him." The other did not share feelings regarding this aspect of his life, except to say that he "did not feel it would be constructive to do so at this point in time."

Adult Relationship

These twins, as they evaluated their relationship with their twin, said they enjoyed being together as they always had.

One twin commented that he still had modest feelings of competitiveness toward this twin. Both of these men said they had, at various times, compared the performance of their children with the children of their twin.

Jerry said this as he reflected upon his life: "I know that I can depend on my twin far more than anyone else in my life, physically, financially, or emotionally. We do not lean on each other, but when we are needed, we are there. It is nice to have that confidence." Don said, "Twinship has had a very positive effect. My family (wife and children) has always loved and been very close to my brother. He is a second husband and father here. My brother's wife has always bitterly opposed our closeness. That has resulted in much strife in his family."

I asked these men if they would like to share any interesting experiences. Don wrote, "There are two things that have shaped my life. One was being a twin and the other was our being so desperately poor as children, we literally huddled together for warmth. That spectre has never left my subconscious nor has the person from where the warmth came."

Their extreme closeness, and the choice of one of them to divorce, due in part to twinship, has meant that his children have missed the presence of their father in the home.

It is impossible to estimate the degree of pain that spouses—and twins—have felt when those who marry a twin do not realize the intense bond that can exist between twins. Identical twins have told me that it is almost like having two husbands, or two wives. Anyone with a jealous nature is sure to have problems marrying an identical twin. Anyone married to a twin should encourage their mate to nourish the relationship with their twin.

Children also suffer when a twin father, or mother, is so devoted to their twin that they neglect to nurture their relationship with their children. Cousins of identical twins are very often extremely close if their twin parents and spouses have a warm and loving relationship with each other.

Advice to Parents of Twins

Don had this to say, "Allow them to do as their inner direction indicates." Jerry commented, "Regarding identical twins, realize that they will see an extension of themselves in the other. Chances are they will be closer to each other than to other siblings."

Because of confidentiality I am unable to share with you greater insight into the pain and anguish that the separated spouse has known, due in part to the closeness of her former husband and the twin brother.

In my other two books I have touched upon the profound effect that twinship can have upon a marriage. I cannot repeat too often the following statement. Anyone who is considering marrying a twin will do themselves and their intended mate an immeasurable favor if they learn all they can about twins and the twin bond.

James and Michael

No other children in the family

I have chosen these men for several reasons. Their birth mother died while giving birth to them. Their father put them up for adoption at the age of six weeks. These men have been instrumental in starting a twin club in their city.

These men are forever grateful that they were not adopted by separate families. Sadly, not all twins have been so fortunate. Recently an eighteen-year-old identical twin appeared on a popular talk show and was reunited with, not only his identical twin brother, but also with his sister and birth mother. Recently this twin had told his adopted mother that he felt he was a twin. On the show he said he had always felt that something was missing from his life. He came to the show not knowing that his twin brother was to come into his life at that time. When his brother appeared, he looked as though he might faint. The host of the show said later that she questioned if she should introduce him to the rest of his family since the initial meeting with his twin brother had come as such a shock.

It is tragic that these twins were denied the joys of growing up together.

Childhood

James and Michael were separated in kindergarten. They recalled being mistaken for one another by teachers and friends.

James says he felt jealous of his twin, and felt he was in competition with him. He also considered himself the leader. Michael did not feel jealous, nor in competition with his twin.

Michael remembered in seventh grade when a nun wanted to separate them. "We were sitting next to each other and she came by and embarrassed us in front of the whole class. She said, 'Are you two married to each other?' I guess she thought we would copy off each other on a test. We didn't like that at all. I guess she didn't realize that we sat next to each other because we just wanted to sit next to each other."

As these twins thought about their childhood they recalled one time when an accident proved just how some twins experience the pain of their twin. Michael wrote, "In the sixth grade my twin hurt his leg really bad. He cut his leg, and we could see the bone. It really freaked us out. It was so weird that while my twin was crying a little, I was the one who was going hysterical. It was strange that I was more upset than he."

Michael said this about school, "Teachers used to mistake us and sometimes got our grades mixed up. When my twin and I were starting college and being rushed to join a fraternity, we were constantly mistaken for one another."

Both saw comparison in a positive way. Michael said "I felt people would compare us, so they could find out the differences between us. Also, I think people compared us because they thought that is what you are supposed to do with twins, to see the similarities and differences between us."

Parent/Child Relationship

As I reviewed the questionnaires of these men I observed that one was much more expressive. They both had comments to make but Michael goes on in much greater detail.

Reflecting back upon the relationship with their parents,

Michael said, "Our parents loved us a lot. We used to have many vacations together. Both our parents treated us the same. They never showed favoritism and treated us as individuals, with proper respect and love. We could not have asked for better parents." Their devotion to their parents is evidenced by an event that took place in 1982. These men have been longtime members of International Twins Association, Inc. Their father died early in the spring of 1982 and they dedicated the 1982 convention to their father.

Adult Relationship

As you read the comments these twins have made about their adult relationship you will see that their minds appear to parallel. It comes as no surprise that these men continue to enjoy a warm and loving relationship with each other as adults. As they reflect on the happy times they now share, they feel that twinship has been a very positive force in their lives.

James says, "Every job we went for, we both got hired. It has definitely been an advantage to go for job interviews together."

Michael said, "Our twinship has definitely helped us in our lifetime. All the jobs we've had, we went together for the interviews and were always hired together. People see twins and think that as a team they would work better together."

James and Michael definitely enjoy being together. They both have degrees in Education and Psychology. They were once employed by the same airline. They both feel twinship has made it easier to find work.

For a long time they held out, saying they did not think they would marry unless they could find twins to marry. They finally changed their minds when the 'right' girls did come along.

Advice to Parents of Twins

James gives this advice, "Let the twins do whatever they want. If they want to dress alike, let them." Michael wrote, "Let them be themselves. If they don't want to dress alike, don't push them.

It is their decision. If they want to, fine. If each wants to go into different activities, let them. Their individuality comes into play now. Treat them fairly and don't favor one of them. Most of all, *love them.*"

Tim and Troy

Two older brothers in family.

I have chosen these men because they feel their twinship has influenced their career paths.

Childhood

These men were dressed alike as little children but did not choose to dress alike as adults. Both felt a degree of competition growing up. Neither felt inferior to the other. They did not feel one was more attractive than the other. They were often mistaken for one another. Both men felt some degree of comparison as children, both by family members and friends. Tim wrote this about comparison, "It created some competitiveness at times— to the extent that each of us would choose opposite paths to avoid the competition." During most of their childhood they shared separate rooms, and always had their own bed.

Tim wrote this about his childhood, "On the positive side, we supported each other and backed up each other in times of duress. We had each other to play with. On the negative side, there was considerable competition for friends and in activities. Our career paths were probably developed to avoid competition. We were often considered to be a 'unit' rather than individuals. We were acknowledged as one-in-the-same. It was sometimes frustrating to have to identify myself from my brother's name."

In thinking about comparison Troy recalled an incident that took place during high school years. "I recall one incident when my twin was selected as a member of the National Honor Society and I was not. The teacher who had the responsibility of telling me this was so apologetic that it was more embarrassing than hurtful or disappointing to me."

Troy wrote this after giving thought about childhood and the positives and negatives of being a twin. "As a twin we were always given special attention, especially in childhood. I think this gave me a sense of feeling special and unique that I have carried into adulthood." He went on to say, "Unfortunately, outside the context of twinhood this has very little relevance and has, at times, created feelings of not being acknowledged enough as a single person/adult. As a result I know some of my behavior has been over dramatized to create attention. This has been a major negative force in my life. In simple words, it seems I have spent much of my life being or trying to be unique or special."

Parent/Child Relationship

The "Yes, No" questions in the Parent/Child section of the questionnaire (located at the back of the book) were identically the same except for question number two, about parental favoritism. Each felt one parent favored one twin, and the other parent favored the other.

Tim wrote, "My father seemed to favor my brother; my mother seemed to favor me. Our personalities were 'matched' in that respect, or perhaps were formulated from it."

Regarding the issue of favoritism, Troy said, "For whatever reason(s) I have always had a strong identification/affinity to my father whereas my twin seemed more in alignment with my mother. In general I have always felt that my mother loved my brother more than me. I never made a big deal of this, however."

Adult Relationship

Here we have two identical twins who not only enjoy being twins, but regret that they live thousands of miles apart.

At this stage in their lives they do not feel any degree of competitiveness. It is understandable that they both feel much closer to one another than they do to other siblings.

Tim says, "I believe twinship has played a big part in my career decisions. I think I chose my career to avoid competition with my brother. I sometimes wonder what direction my life would have taken without my brother's influence."

Tim wrote that recently he and his twin were talking about their vocational choices. He said, "I was telling him about my bifurcation into the sciences as a result of his choice to pursue the arts. He then admitted that he was often envious of my pursuits of the science, (hence has recently taken up a vocation requiring knowledge of the health sciences) and I admitted to him that I got into my artistic explorations by creative research and writing, poetry, woodworking and jewelry designs. As they say, what goes around, comes around. I close by saying that I feel blessed and privileged to be a twin, especially with Troy. I have an opportunity to experience life noticeably different from most siblings. In this way it feels good to be 'different.' It feels good to be a twin."

Troy remarked that he had always struggled for independence from his brother and from being a twin. He now feels that this position has cost him dearly in terms of intimacy with his brother and he added, "as I get older I regret this much more."

Troy wrote, "Comparisons in twinhood are a given—perhaps more than the typical sibling, in that the standards of judgment are more tightly woven on a psychic rather than a social level. The competition factor colored my whole self-perception as having an ambiguous, if not split, identity. The insidious part was not always due to 'outside' pressure or influence of parents, family, peers, etc; but rather from the inner sanctuary of my own psyche. My self esteem was the target. I forgot who I was because I had a brother who seemed to 'know' or be more focused on a career at an earlier age than I. It appeared quite clear that by age fourteen, he had decided on a professional career. He sought out academic work (science) to support that interest. I remember feeling inadequate because I did not know my destiny. When asked what I was going to do in the future I was typically embarrassed and would often respond by telling them what my twin was going to do. (It got me off the hook.) I somehow felt alienated from my twin. I also had thought there was not enough 'room' or space (i.e., too much competition) for both of us to share the same interests, much less endeavor. I often sought out different friends and activities for this reason.

"I was never jealous of his choices, only envious that I did not have the focus or career commitment at that age. Although he had the career in mind, I had only the energy. And a lot of it! (Competition does breed energy.) When we had completed high school we took off in high gear to pursue our individual goals. We selected different colleges some 1,500 miles apart.

"Since my brother was determined to seek a profession in a science-based field (optometry), I sought a different path...one that would not compete with his. I reluctantly pursued a background in liberal arts and visual arts. The idea of pursuing a field of expression appealed to me as it was intuitive and allowed for a soft-edge interpretation of reality and a subjective point of view. In a sense it opposed science. Through the influence of an older brother I woke to the reality of art and it became my passion, my purpose. I taught for several years but the passion for painting opened the vistas of my mind that no one could reach, understand, condemn or *compare*. Subjective reality became a safe haven for me. I could be who I was without a reference to anyone, including a twin. It satisfied to some degree an inner need to express, experiment and define a world of illusion on my own terms. I chose my own language, my own symbols, and my own identity. It became a concept for me in several sculptures, paintings and journal writings. A personal challenge became one of making a beautiful statement about the process of creation. I was on my own path. Finally.

"At no time did I ever want to undermine my brother's work. As a matter of fact, I was extremely proud of his academic accomplishments and looked forward to reuniting with him from time to time. Although we were many physical miles apart there was never a time when I felt he was more than a second away. If anything, *his* success was an impetuous for my own motivation. Although our worlds seemed far apart, the drive to achieve and get recognition was sparked by my twin's accomplishments.

"A second factor affecting my career determination had to do with family finances/resources available for higher education. There was stress since there was a single income that was inconsistant and unpredictable. This was not fully understood at the time. It had a significant effect on both our educational goals as there were two individuals starting college at the same time— a considerable expense.

"My brother has told me on occasion that he experienced some guilt because of the financial limitations. For me it became a matter of *whose* career would be more valuable (deserving). At that time his career demanded more financial support because he was becoming a 'Dr.' and tuition costs were markedly higher. It became my perception that the resources available should go to him, and that I would have to find another way. I did not see this as a sacrifice on any conscious level although on a very subtle level I began to see myself as something less than he and consequently less deserving. To compensate, I became more determined to establish my self worth by setting extremely high standards and expectations. When those expectations were not met it often meant more self incrimination. A vicious cycle of chasing my tail began and a self-defeating perception developed which took many years to undo.

"Resentment on the other hand seemed to operate on a much deeper layer of my psyche. Those feelings that were not appropriately expressed manifested themselves in a kind of anger/ resentment that colored my perception in darkness. This I experienced in many ways, namely in relationships with significant others. The fear of being judged/compared was paramount for me. It followed me like a shadow. I felt this more intensely in my relationship with my mother when she spoke of her 'Dr.' son. Somehow I never felt as if I 'measured up' to my twin brother in my parents' eyes. It was not until my parents were deceased that my mind was healed of this illusion."

Troy concluded his letter to me by adding, "It is interesting to note that my mother had a twin sister (non-identical) and I am a father of boy/girl twins. No doubt we teach what we have learned from our past, so it has become a challenge raising my own children consciously clear and free of twin trappings. I talk with my twins often about 'twinship' in hopes that communication can ward off unhealthy behavior patterns that can be formed as a result of being a twin.

(I asked my daughter, age fourteen, what she thought of this subject and her response was interesting. She requested a different high school than her twin brother. Individuality without alienation was her goal.) Cool!"

The letter from Troy was long but worthy of being included in its entirety. His exploration into his twinship feelings surely has not only been a catharsis for him in finding peace within himself, but has served in making the bond between him and his twin brother even more secure.

Tim was also kind enough to put in writing his thoughts about how twinship may have played a part in his choice of vocation. Tim wrote, "The first recollection of any singular influence on my vocational choice goes back to an event when my brother and I were some five or six years of age. We were drawing and coloring when my older brother came into the house. (He was ten years our senior, an artist, and in many ways was more of a father figure than my dad.) We both showed him our drawings and I remember very distinctly that Troy got more praise/ acknowledgment/attention than I did. An authoritative person had spoken! I felt 'crushed' by this and went upstairs and threw my crayolas around the room! I don't recall pursuing drawing (the arts) for years for some reason(s). I had just not felt I was 'good' enough; certainly not as good as my twin. Troy, to this day, is indeed a very fine artist. In retrospect I am sure there was no purposeful ploy from my older brother to quell my artistic talents. In fact, it could have been that Troy got the attention because his work was inferior to mine and thusly, he needed the additional attention. It is fun to think of the various spins such as this. As far as any influences from my parents with regards to vocational choices, I am left with the feeling and impression that it didn't really matter as long as I was doing what I wanted.

"I cannot end without commenting on what I believe to be major 'ingredients' in my vocational choice and which has also extended into my other life choices. These ingredients include such concepts as competitiveness, identity (self awareness), uniqueness and autonomy. In order to achieve a separateness from my twin I believe I purposefully made choices that I might not have made otherwise. For example, if my brother was to pursue the arts, then I would pursue the sciences, which is what we actually did. I would learn to choose different friends, different clothing, different sports, different interests, different differences in my attempt to be different. This would minimize the competition. This would minimize the lack of identity of being called Troy/Tim, the boys, even 'hey you, whichever one you are.' I do believe at both conscious and subconscious levels, I made life choices on these bases."

Advice to Parents

Troy offered this advice to parents of twins, "Perhaps it is a bit easier for me to offer advice since I am the father of boy/girl twins. Some of the problems I have experienced still remain…How do I support these two independent bodies that share a special bond? I would suggest: Develop them as individuals to the greatest extent possible, but impress upon them their twin heritage/lineage and the specialness of having the unique other. Nurture this in sharing ways (twin clubs, organizations, conventions, etc.) Try to bring some balance and harmony into this unique relationship by stressing the importance of acceptance. Be proud of oneself and the other one.

"Finally, in an effort to promote separate identities, I think it is important to spend as much time possible with both twins individually. Sometimes there is more affinity with one or the other but attention should be to the other. I have learned, however, that it is not always possible to be 'fair' or 'equal' all of the time. This should be carved in stone."

Tim's advice to parents of twins is this, "It is difficult to give absolute direction and advice to parents of twins as to how to deal with these issues. There is much innocence/naivete associated with it and there are specific situations where twins really prefer the closeness of being 'one and inseparable.' I believe parents should become educated as to the issues involving twinships, from all the angles, and pay attention to their own twins' behavior and interactions. Good communication at as early of an age as possible seems appropriate. Try to get some idea how each twin feels about his need for autonomy/similarity and proceed from there. This needs to be assessed from time to time, as our needs change as we get older. Information and education are the key operatives here."

George and Wayne

These men come from a very large family. They have nine older brothers, four older sisters, one younger brother and two younger sisters.

As you read about the twins in this book, I'm sure you will recognize that life does not always seem fair. With one set of twins I tell how they were adopted into a supportive and harmonious family. Yet, you read of this set of twins who was abandoned at birth and later adopted into a family where there was discord and unhappiness for the twin children.

From the over 800 twins I researched, only three sets of twins did not know which was born first. Two of these sets did not know because they were adopted and did not have their birth records. Such is the case with these men who are ordained ministers.

Childhood

They grew up in a large two-parent family, but say their childhood did not offer emotional security. They attended the same school and were in most of the same classrooms until the seventh grade. They remember being dressed alike as small children and often chose to dress alike when older, especially when performing. George considered himself the leader. They were often mistaken for one another. As children, one of them felt jealousy toward his twin, as well as inferior to his twin. They did not feel they were compared and had no comments to make regarding comparison.

As these men reflected back upon their childhood and the positives and negatives as a twin growing up, George told me, "The positive aspect was that we were so very competitive, and that encouraged us to work harder. We paced one another constantly. The negative aspect was, I often got taken, or should I say mistaken, for my twin. That wasn't good because he was a flirt with the girls and that quite often got me into trouble, because my girlfriend wanted to know why I was flirting with another girl. Only my twin had that answer."

Wayne wrote this about the positives and negatives he felt as he reflected back upon his childhood years, "My twin was always there to help me when I got in trouble. It was nice to know my twin would be there. When I think of the negative the only thing I can think of are the two black eyes I received when I called him a name that he disliked."

Parent/Child Relationship

These men felt no favoritism was shown by either parent. They both recall being given derogatory names by their parents. They also felt that punishment was not administered fairly by their parents. These men recall they were not encouraged to participate in any extra-curricular activities.

George had this to say about his relationship with his foster parents, "We lived in constant fear of being threatened that if we were not good, they would send us away to a mental institution or reform school. We were battered children and lived under much ridicule. We feel no bitterness toward them. The proper attitude is simply sadness. Our real parents abandoned us at birth."

Wayne shared this about his relationship with his parents, "We were often beaten and battered. We did not have a happy home. If there was such thing called happiness, we never saw it or knew it existed. I wish they could have treated us with love. I envied other families that showed love and got involved with one another. My twin and I both missed that."

Adult Relationship

These men both agree that they enjoy being with each other most of the time, and the closeness they feel toward each other becomes tighter as they grow older. Both of them agree that they still feel a high degree of competitiveness toward one another. As one said, "We pace one another as we jog together."

They both admit to having a much closer relationship with one another than they do with other siblings.

In response to the question I asked regarding twinship and the possible effect it may have had upon each of their lives, George said, "In many ways it can be a real exposure of plusses, yet on the other hand it can be a real detrimental blow to either should one of us do anything that would harm the other's image. We are so similar, yet so very, very different. People who know me well can see the difference in personality."

Wayne wrote, "We have helped one another so much. If it weren't for my twin I would not have become a minister. Being a twin has had a great effect upon my life. We are our own selves first. We have our own identities, yet our interests are the same and dislikes the same. Twinship has been a blessing 98 percent of the time."

Advice to Parents of Twins

George gives parents the following advice, "Love them and nurture them in an atmosphere of encouragement. Teach them to be kind and work with them both. Never compare them to each other, unless there's a positive outcome to be expected."

Wayne said, "Encourage them and help them to help one another. Show them that they are two different people who just happen to bear the same identical resemblance. Don't favor one over the other."

Richard & Roland Marshall

These twins had one older sister in family.

I chose this set of twins to show you the extreme closeness these twins felt as children and how their tight bond brought them together after retirement. *Author's note: Richard and Roland were asked to give an update on their relationship during research for this book. Shortly after Richard replied, he passed away. A tribute to them will be found in Chapter Eleven. The names used are their own names.*

Childhood

These men were in the same classroom all through school. They were separated when both were commissioned as Naval aviators in 1942. They shared many of the same playmates, were dressed alike as children and chose to dress alike when older. They were not jealous of one another, nor did either feel inferior to the other. They were most often mistaken for one another.

Richard did state that he sometimes felt in competition with his brother, and sometimes felt he was not as smart as his twin. He stated this regarding comparison with his brother: "It hurt at times. My twin was smart. He always applied himself and studied hard. I wanted to play a little more but felt I had to keep up with him." Richard did not consider himself the leader.

Roland did feel competition with his brother during childhood. He did not feel less smart, nor inferior to his twin. He did feel that they were both often compared by family members and friends. He made these comments: "This did not bother me. We knew we were in competition with one another, consequently we both studied and were both honor students and lived up to what was expected of us."

These are Richard's comments as he reflected back upon his childhood: "We attended the same college together. Examinations were given in a big gymnasium. I couldn't even see where he was sitting. We would both miss the same questions on the exam. At graduation time we received a joint award for high scholastic standing. First time that had been done at the college. We were roomates, too, which kept the competition keen."

Roland said this as he looked back over the childhood years. "Having a twin was great. We were very close and still maintain a great relationship today.'

Parent/Child Relationship

Neither of these men felt their parents showed any favoritism toward them. They both readily admit to their parents comparing their performance with one another. Both said they were encouraged to develop their own extra-curricular activities.

Adult Relationship

Both of these men said they enjoy being with their twin and that the feeling of closeness has become even stronger as they have grown older. Neither one now has any feelings of competitiveness toward the other.

Richard said this as he thought about life lived as a twin: "We have had happy times together. There was always the competitive feeling and striving for excellence."

Roland shared this after reflecting upon his life with a twin brother. "I never felt alone, because I had a special brother to share growing up experiences with each day. My mother dressed us alike, and then when we went into aviation flight school the Navy dressed us alike."

Advice to Parents of Twins

Richard offered this advice, "Do not keep comparing every thing they do. Let them develop individual interests."

Roland said, "Equal treatment for each."

Interesting Experiences

Richard wrote, "Even at age sixty, sometimes I feel I am my brother. After thirty-five years separated, we now live close and can share our lives again. Most of our grandchildren live close by, too."

Roland shared this, "During the war (WWII) I was flying in the Pacific and my brother was flying in South America. A few of my brother's squadron officers were transferred to Honolulu and thought I was my brother. In college we traded dates without the girls being aware of the switch. An advantage of being a twin is that you can always prove you were somewhere else."

Author's note: You will read more about Richard and Roland Marshall in Chapter Eleven.

Chapter Three

Identical Women

Ruth and Dorothy

These women were adopted at birth and raised together.
Double wedding ceremony-one lasted, one ended in divorce.
No other siblings.

How many people can say that in adulthood they found two families? There are two events that have greatly enriched the lives of these two women. One is when they discovered the International Twins Association (ITA), a yearly gathering of twins that they refer to as their second family. Secondly, they found their biological mother.

These women are picture perfect. I first met them at the annual twins convention that is always held somewhere in the United Stated over Labor Day weekend. They were identical in every way: clothing identical, hair style the same, even the same smile. I soon learned they didn't mind if I got their names mixed—so typical of the feelings of some identical twins.

Seeing these two together and observing their identical mannerisms was another lesson for me in how alike twins can be. Not only was I surprised at the synchronization, but even more surprised when one of them said to me, "We always amaze ourselves by how many times we say exactly the same thing or are reminded of the same idea at the same time."

The greatest joy these women have known was the day they found their birthmother. They started their search in 1977. They found her the day before Mother's Day 1979. Ruth had this to say, "Finding our birthmother was the best thing that ever happened to us." Dorothy said, "My mind still whirls in amazement when I think of the joy of finding our birthmother."

Childhood

These women gave this information about their childhood: They attended the same school, and were in the same class through the sixth grade. They shared many of the same playmates, were dressed alike as small children and continued to always dress alike. They celebrated birthdays together, were not jealous of their twin, and did not feel in competition with one another. They did not feel inferior to each other, nor less smart. They were often mistaken for one another and felt compared by family members and friends.

Here is what Ruth had to say about comparison: "I don't think I minded being compared in order to help others tell us apart, but I wish they had picked a positive difference instead of negative. The negative examples were freckles on the nose or fatter face."

Ruth made this comment, "Some people could never tell us apart, while others could easily distinguish one from the other. We usually pointed out our own differences, so I suppose it wasn't a problem."

Parent/Child Relationship

Dorothy said, "Our adopted mother died when we were seven. Our adopted father married thirteen months later. We feel we parented ourselves.

Our parents isolated and overprotected us from the world. Therefore, we were pathetically shy and still are unable to

socialize. Our parents never gave us the opportunity to choose
for ourselves or make our own decisions. They never gave us the
ability to have confidence in ourselves. Our parents were very
close-minded and never allowed us to ask any curious questions
of a sexual nature.

"We never dated until age twenty-two. Our dad used to joke
about keeping a baseball bat at the front door to keep guys away.
It worked!"

Ruth said, "During the first seven years of our lives, we were
our adoptive parents' only children. They were much older than
the average parents, and even though they overprotected us, they
did want us. After our adoptive mother died, our stepmother
became upset when she couldn't understand our head-to-head
conversations with each other. Our twinship didn't have anything
to do with the zero communication between our parents and us.
We didn't get any support or encouragement from our parents.
I'm surprised I continued to play violin because my stepmother
hated for me to practice in my bedroom and she refused to come
to any of my concerts or listen to me play in church. Because she
wouldn't come, my dad didn't want to make waves so he never
heard me perform either, even when I was in college and played
in a state university symphony orchestra."

Ruth said, "Since my twin and I were adopted, at least I had
someone in the family I was physically related to. I don't feel I
had a very close relationship with my parents even though we
were together as a family every day. Our parents didn't teach us
to think for ourselves, nor did they encourage us to develop
opinions and discuss issues. I remember as a teenager
(approximately fourteen years old) asking my father what an
abortion was. He couldn't or wouldn't tell me and I quickly
learned never to ask another question."

One of the questions non-twins wonder about twins (even
some twins), is whether they really do have Extra Sensory
Perception. These women are representative of many of the
identical women (and men) who have told me of the workings of
ESP in their lives.

They enjoy telling of the time when one was out salmon

fishing on the ocean with her husband. One of them became seasick and later learned that her twin, who was taking a shower at the same time, almost fainted.

They tell me they amaze themselves at the many times they express the same idea at the same time. These women live approximately one hundred miles apart and talk on the phone frequently. When they ask what the other is wearing, they often find they are wearing identical outfits, or have fixed the same menu for dinner. I've observed that many identical women, when shopping, will buy an identical outfit for their twin.

Adult Relationship

Their responses to the questions regarding their adult relationship were identical. They enjoy being with their twin. They feel no competitiveness toward their twin.

These women are surprised they are married, since they were so happy as twins.

Here is what each of them had to say regarding their relationship as an adult.

Ruth wrote: "When I was the first one to date my future husband, I felt like I was abandoning my best friend. There is nothing better than being a twin. I wish God had made everyone a twin.

Dorothy wrote: "I am the more liberal of the two, so if I were a singleton, possibly I wouldn't have felt the constraint of my more conservative twin. Because we had only each other as friends and the fact that we're extremely introverted and have inferiority complexes, I'm amazed we didn't remain single and live together all our lives."

Advice to Parents of Twins

Ruth wrote: "Let the twins decide if they want to do things together, dress alike, etc., when they are old enough to do so."

Dorothy said: "Let them make their own decisions whether to dress alike, attend the same classes, study the same subjects, enjoy the same hobbies, or learn the same musical instrument."

As we close with this set of twins, I do think it is interesting that the handwriting of each of these twins is almost identical. Their signatures are identical except different spellings. Perhaps someday someone will research the handwriting of twins.

How do these twins feel about being twins? They expressed the feelings of many twins when they made the following statements: "My twin is always there to understand and support me. We'd probably give our lives for each other, but no one else, not even a spouse."

Rachel and Karen

No other siblings in the family

I chose to tell you about these identical twins for several reasons. I lived in the same town as these girls when they were growing up. We attended the same church, which gave me the opportunity to observe them. At that time I saw them as others did, two little girls who were always together, who always dressed alike, and two little girls who seemed to be happy all the time.

These women were thirty-nine years old when they took part in my research. I've had the pleasure of following their lives since 1984 and seeing the shape their lives have taken; observing all the while the part twinship has played in it.

As they were growing up, they took part in many local functions, dancing or appearing on television. Their total identity was "The Smith Twins."

Childhood

All of the yes/no questions that were asked in the questionnaire elicited identical responses from these two women, even though they were filled out apart from one another.

They were in the same classes at school until the seventh grade. They always dressed alike and continued to do so throughout their school years. They were never jealous of one another, nor did they feel in competition with each other. One did not feel inferior to the other, nor less smart. They took turns being leader and follower.

They did not feel compared, but one did remember relatives commenting on how alike they appeared to be.

When I asked them to sum up memories of their childhood they had this to say:

Karen wrote: "I honestly can't think of one negative part of being a twin. The positive, you have a close friend for life. You understand each other completely. You have a friend to share all the emotional and trying times. You can be totally honest with your twin—if you're not they know you're lying. You have a playmate that shares your interests and talents. You have fun mixing people up. You get lots of attention. Twins have the advantage of being special from birth on—you don't have to 'earn' being special! Being a twin is safe. You never have to worry about being left out of 'the' group. Especially during early teen years where being accepted is so important. You are not alone. What security!"

Rachel wrote: "We were always 'on show.' We danced or performed on TV and at local functions several times a week. Our total identity was 'The Smith Twins.' After twenty years of living away, I am still stopped by people and recognized. I suppose this is a positive aspect. We were *definitely* popular—partly because of being twins. We dressed exactly alike until we graduated from high school. We enjoyed this. Now we occasionally choose to dress alike for special occasions—anniversaries, reunions, etc."

Parent/Child Relationship

They were the only children in the family, the apple of their parents' eye, yet it was the mother who took exceptional pride in the fact that "her girls were twins." It was most important they be dressed impeccably, as well as being dressed exactly alike in every detail. As one of these women wrote, "Our mother emphasized putting us 'on stage' all the time. We were not just her children...we were hers, to "show off." She made a production of getting us ready for people to see...whether we were just shopping or going on stage in a performance." "But...if you asked us what we would have had mother do differently...we would also say *nothing!!!* Our greatest joy in life has been being identical twins. We would not trade wisdom, talent or fortunes for the experience we've been able to share...and will continue to share."

Their father made no effort to tell them apart; in fact I always chuckle when I think of one event that took place when they were small. One of the girls told me, "I remember one time when he gave me a spanking...only to discover my twin should have been spanked... His comment was, "Well, you look more like Rachel than Rachel does."

These women felt no favoritism by either parent. Never did they feel any comparison was made between them.

These women grew up in a loving and secure environment. They knew their boundaries and respected them. Karen said, "The strongest rule in our house was—' You are never allowed to fight or argue with each other or with your parents.'" We grew up believing that and never really had a fight. There may be some problems with that for others but for us it worked perfectly."

Their parents insisted they share everything completely and equally. Karen said, "If one baby-sat, we automatically gave one-half of the earnings to the other. Even in our adult life we share. If one has financial problems the other sends money...and we don't keep track of it."

To let you readers know this has continued on in their life, I'll let Karen tell you about their recent trip to Europe. "Only six weeks ago (as almost 44-year-old twins) when we were sitting next to each other and about to land in England, she asked me how much money I had. Would you believe we divided our money so we'd be equal! Will it ever end? I certainly hope not!"

Adult Relationship

These women were emphatic when I asked them if they still enjoyed being with their twin. I knew what their response would be—and what it will always be. These women feel complete when they are with their twin. Karen expressed her feelings by saying, "What a void I would have in my life if I couldn't spend time with my 'best friend.'" Rachel said "I can't imagine what it would be like not to have a twin. I think I would feel less secure and less self-confident. I would have had to work harder to attain the same success. As a teacher I was even hired by a principal who knew me as one of the 'twins.' We share something special I wish everyone had a chance to share... "

Rachel recalls "As children we didn't develop close girl friend relationships because we had each other. I was thirty-three years old before I had a close female friend. People expect us to be wonderful as a twin—so I have to also be wonderful as a single."

These women have both taught school and are now retired. They are both professional artists. They are married and each has one daughter. They live 170 miles apart and tell me they call one another two or three times almost every day.

You will read more about these twins' feelings about their marriage relationships in a later chapter.

Advice to Parents of Twins

Rachel said, "Just roll with the punches. If the twins want to be together and be alike, let them. If they want to be individuals, let them. Take your clues from the twins."

Karen said, "Let them love one another...give them the opportunity to develop a special relationship. Don't try to force identical twins to be different from each other. Encourage twins to share something special they can't share with anyone else in the family."

Nancy and Iris

No other siblings in the family

"I've always wanted twins." This comment has often been made to me when I've let it be known I am a twin researcher. It would be nice to think having twins is always the ideal way to have babies, but the mother of this twin set is quick to say having twins is a greater handicap than one can imagine. I spent over an hour with the mother of these twins and she expressed her feelings openly and with deep sincerity.

These identical twin girls were sixteen when they first took part in my research. I've followed them for twelve years and it's been interesting to see their life patterns emerge.

Their father is a professional man; their mother a homemaker. They grew up in a secure family setting. However, their father being a professional man was away from home much of the time, which left a great deal of the childrearing to the mother.

After talking at great length with the mother of these girls, I believe she might well think they fought even in utero.

Even at the age of sixteen these girls were expressive and able to tell how they felt about being twins, even though they said they had not given much thought about the effects of twinship upon their lives.

Childhood

They attended the same school but were not in class together. They did not dress alike as children, nor as adults. They were often mistaken for one another. Iris was jealous of her twin and felt in competition with her. She also felt inferior to her twin and considered herself to be less attractive. She also felt dominated by her twin.

One of these girls wrote at length about competition. It is lengthy, but I include it because it has a powerful message to parents of twins.

Nancy wrote, "There is also a question of competition among twins that starts with the names they are given at birth. For example when a twin is given an identical twin as a sibling, then given a name that does not exactly set her apart from her identical twin, (i.e., Don and Ron, Sharon and Karen, etc.) it sets her up for some immediate competition.

There are some kinds of competition that are considered good, and some that are considered bad, or unhealthy. The type of competition involved in a twin relationship is not any of these. The competition a twin feels is strictly a fight for her independence, and for singular recognition by parents and friends. There is nothing good or bad, healthy or unhealthy about twin competition. The child simply learns at an unusually young age, how to compete for the feelings a single child would feel at the same young age: the feeling there is an identity that is distinctive only to that one child.

There is no need for the single child to 'prove' to anyone they are the one and only special person in their parents' lives. There is a feeling, bordering on self-preservation, that a twin feels naturally, from the time she starts to interact with people. It is a feeling she must win the affections of family, friends, and anyone who matters in her life. This feeling is similar to the feeling the prospective employee might feel during a job interview. Impress and charm. In some cases, at any cost. For twins, it can result in carefully, oh-so-subtly, making your twin look less favorable in comparison. Once again, this feeling is not intentional. It is a natural feeling that comes on so gradually, it is difficult to control.

I think when talking about twins, the correct term to use is not, 'Is there any competition?' but rather, 'What are the comparisons?' It is my belief that those are two key words in discussing a twin relationship. The two C's, if you will: competition and comparison."

When asked about comparison, Nancy said, "Most people knew we were trying to establish separate personalities. They didn't usually compare us. Our parents never did."

Iris said, "I felt we were being compared (by parents) on an academic level. Now I know this is not true. By friends, I felt we were being compared to see who was more progressive."

They discussed positive and negatives about their childhood as twins. Nancy said, "There was always someone to do things with and to talk to. But we got into fights a lot." Iris said, "The negative was, I was always worried about who got more love and attention, etc. Positive things are that even though we fought, and still do, we had a head start on our sisterly relationship."

As I reviewed their questionnaires, I found that the twin who felt less threatened by twinship, was also the one who worried a great deal about who was getting the most love and attention from parents.

Parent/Child Relationship

These women did not feel their parents favored one over the other. They felt they were treated equally. They said their parents encouraged them to develop their own interests and to participate in extracurricular activities of their choice.

Iris did state when they were quite small their father was almost never home. She said, "We sort of had to build on our father/daughter relationship when older."

Nancy said, "I feel I have to be someone completely different—even if sometimes it's really not me."

Adult Relationship

Five years after first meeting these young women I went to them again, asking them to go into greater detail about their relationship with each other.

Nancy had this to say about her twinship. Her feelings express similar thoughts that I've heard from others. As you read her comments you will find that, if she could do it all over, she'd try to be more understanding, and more compassionate with her twin.

"The word "twin" brings to mind many different adjectives: confusing, interesting, maddening, and wonderful are a few that just scratch the surface.

"Being someone's exact mirror image is quite a strange thing to live with, and when so many people try so hard to look like one another, i.e., 'wannabees,' it's hard for a twin to understand that desire.

"I suppose the difficulty arises in the fact that two separate people, two entirely different entities or identities, look exactly alike! Society has a way of looking upon twins as *one* human being—easily understood—they look like one therefore they are one, right? *Wrong!* Most twins are really very different people, and when two different, separate individuals are treated as one, the natural response is to impress upon others how different you *really are*. This often leads to a 'itty bit' of emotional difficulty.

"To 'prove' (for lack of a better word) that you're not her and she's not you, one goes to great lengths—in attitudes and styles, for instance; punk vs. preppy, prude vs. loose (in theory, of course, not practice), and every other expression of one's individuality that can be pulled to opposite ends of the 'expressionary spectrum.'

"To start out as a twin, as a young child with no bias, and no cares in the world except to be loved by those around you, is a *wonderful* experience! Here you are, a new little person, with a built-in playmate, always close by. How comforting! If mommy and daddy are not right there when you see that great big purple, one-eyed monster under your bed, *she* is. You aren't afraid of being alone—your twin is always there. The two of you share toys, uncover the world, refine your motor skills, and generally learn about life, *together* with a ready-made support network right there for you, watching, learning, growing, helping, right alongside you. What an exciting way to start a new life!

"Unfortunately, that wonderful time did not last forever. My twin and I grew up and learned (whether taught by society, or just evolving into this way of thinking), that twins must share everything. This does not present a problem where material things are concerned, but suddenly, there is a realization that affection and attention must be shared. That's when jealousy rears up its nasty, ugly head, and emotional strain paints itself into the 'twin' picture and makes it an ugly one dimensional picture.

"Without a doubt, this problem does not present itself to all twins, but that small percentage that *do* have trouble sharing emotions from others find it a hard hurdle to cross.

"While I was growing up, I found the way to 'get one up' on my twin (in terms of receiving more attention and affection) was to 'knock her down' one emotional rung after another. As the saying goes—the truth hurts. If I could lie, and say this never occurred, I might feel better—but it did. I pushed to be the first one to do things, learn new skills, take risks—to be the brave one. I wanted to be the better of us, and when my twin followed my lead and tried these new things, I made sure she was not much of a success. I was always there for her emotionally, but indirectly made sure she was second best by *my* being the best. *Not* a very nice thing to do, I know, but when faced with the thought of being second best to someone so much like you, one is willing to do almost anything.

"When I think back on all the times I could have been more of a support to her instead of a stumbling block, and the things we could have accomplished and overcome together—I feel a deep sense of loss. What a unit of two so closely bonded people can do together, is boundless. This is why I feel so strongly about informing other twins of the great things you can do together. Twins have two angles on *everything*, and almost always know what the other is thinking. The possibilities are limitless.

"When my twin left for college, I had a difficult time dealing with her absence. Being separated from someone with whom you shared a womb is a bit of an adjustment.

"In retrospect, I wish I had treated my twin with more respect and love. I think we could have accomplished a great deal together—much more than we did. It could have been constructive instead of destructive."

Advice to Parents of Twins

Nancy gives this advice: "Don't encourage them to be the same. Help them to be different.

"As far as advice to parents goes, I just want any parent out there to know they have my sympathy. Don't dress your twins in identical clothing. Aside from any future effects on the kids, you yourself will get confused. When twins are dressed exactly alike they lose their identity. Try to discourage comparison of each other between the twins. This comparing yourself to your twin does carry over to real life, and leads you to compare yourself to everyone around you. This is something I am guilty of. Learn to compare yourself to you. Evaluate yourself this year in light of what you were last year."

Iris encourages parents to: "... *constantly* give each the *same* amount of affection, and involve each of them in *totally* different activities."

Alice and Clarice

(At their request, these names were not changed.) No other siblings in the family

Of all the twin sets I researched, perhaps it is this set of twins that made me realize just how alike some twins can be.

Their questionnaires reached my mailbox at the same time. I read the first with great intrigue, but the intrigue was intensified as I read the identical material in the second letter. They were exactly alike! Fascinating, I thought. Can twins really be this in tune with one another? Are they really being themselves, or just trying to mimic one another in all ways? I had to find out.

Due to my extensive research, phone bills are enormous, so I try to do my calling earlier or later in the day, but my curiosity outweighed my sense of thrift. I went immediately to the phone and called this fascinating set of twins. Not one but two answered the phone. Is this Clarice, I asked? Yes, but Alice is on the other phone. Of course, I might have known.

When I called, they were surprised to find me at the other end of the line. "Your questionnaires just came to me and I must ask you, did you fill them out independently?" Being totally honest they both replied, "No, we did them together, but they would have been the same even if we had done them separately." "Would they really?" I thought. Now I've come to believe that yes, they probably would have been identical had they filled them out separately.

I told them I was shocked to find such alikeness. At this point I was early on in my research, with much yet to learn about twins. Since I had never found such a degree of alikeness I didn't want to convey to them my real thoughts, such as, "I think they're weird." Let me hasten to say that over the years I've come to know these twins personally and must say I've never met more charming women and totally happy people than these two.

Wow, I thought, this will be interesting reading for people who want to know how alike twins can be, but I questioned "Will they let me tell their story publicly?" Since I was learning that research demands you be somewhat bold as you seek greater understanding of a subject, I told myself this is what I must do.

When I asked these twins if I could share what they had told me, *they* said, "Only if you use our names together, not separately." Fair enough, I thought, so let me now tell you what they told me. It's interesting!

Childhood

I found these facts about their childhood as I read their questionnaires:

1. They grew up in a loving family with one sister. They were always together in the classroom, including college.

2. They always shared the same playmates, always dressed alike and were always given the same gifts.

3. They never considered one the leader. They were never jealous of each other, nor did they feel in competition. They never felt one was being compared with the other.

4. They never felt inferior to one another, nor felt one was smarter.

5. They were often mistaken by friends and family.

When they were asked to tell their feelings about the treatment they were given as children by family and friends they said, "We felt the same. In fact, we feel like *one* person and we like it!"

I asked them to give any positives or negatives they felt about being a twin; they had this to say, "We think it's *great* and we're very lucky; there are no negatives."

Parent/Child Relationship

Children are greatly influenced by the attitudes parents have toward each of their children. The relationships that develop between parents of twins are going to be different from relationships between siblings because they are dealing with not one, but two at the same time.

It matters greatly how parents of twins see their twin children—as individuals or as a pair. How twins perceive their parents' attitude toward them will have a lifelong effect on how twins feel about themselves and about their twin.

Let me share with you how these twins felt about their relationship with their parents as they were growing up.

1. Their parents showed no favoritism.

2. They, nor their performance were ever compared with one another.

3. They were free to choose their own activities.

About their childhood relationship with their parents they wrote: "Our family always treated us the same. They dressed us alike, then when we were old enough to choose, they let us make all decisions as far as being twins was concerned; dressing alike, same room at school, same bedroom, same interests, etc. We are very happy, and we think *all* twins should have the right to choose for themselves."

Adult Relationship

We now look into the adult relationship of these twins, who are in their late fifties.

They say:
1. We always enjoy being with one another.
2. We feel no competitiveness with one another.
3. We feel we know each other very well.
4. We have a closer relationship with each other than we do with our sibling.

When asked to comment about their twinship and the effects of twinship upon their lives, they wrote:
"We have *never* been separated! We cannot imagine *not* being twins. We are extremely happy, and always have been. We would not change a thing! We feel much more fulfilled for having been born a twin."

When asked if there were any interesting experiences they would like to share they wrote, "Our whole life is a happy interesting experience, and being lucky enough to be twins has made it doubly so."

These women had this to say about individuality and twins:
"This is a 'sore subject' with us. We're tired of reading and hearing about 'individuality'. Society can help by leaving twins to do what they wish, and society should not tell twins what to do. We are what we are, and *no* one has a right to advise us. Other people do not understand. We personally have not been bothered by this kind of thinking, because we had a chance to choose. But it worries us (no small amount) that some other twins may be affected by this 'individuality' thinking, and may never have the opportunity to be as happy as we."

These twins thanked me for including them in the research and for giving them the opportunity to express their feelings.

These women are concert piano-duettists. They have toured extensively and won remarkable acclaim from audiences and critics for their musical integrity, their technique, and their charm. They are billed as The Rainer Twins—One Piano, Four Hands.

Advice to Parents of Twins

These twins were delighted to have a chance to express their views on twinship and how they feel parents of twins should treat their twin children. In their words they wrote:

"Treat them exactly alike and dress them alike. Let them share everything until they are old enough to decide what they want. Let the twins decide. *No* one else knows how they feel.

"We find it extremely hard to understand why twins would have problems with being twins. It is our opinion that twins would not have any problems with being twins unless other people cause the problems."

Sally and Sue

No other siblings in the family

Meet identical twin women who were in their mid-thirties when we first met. They were very excited about being a part of my research, and went deep into their experiences in hopes of learning as much as they could to better understand their twin relationship. Their thoughtful answers reveal the great complexity twinship can have.

Both of these twins feel they are especially interesting from a psychological viewpoint since their lives are so completely opposite. (Remember, we are talking about their lives as they were in the early 1980s.)

Sally writes, "I am the single career woman and she, the homemaker with three children. It was chance, not choice, for both of us!"

Childhood

They were in the same classroom until seventh grade. They dressed alike as small children but dressed differently as they grew older. Their playmates were often shared. These women were often jealous of their twin and felt in competition with one another. They were often mistaken for the other. Both felt inferior to their twin, and felt they were compared by family members and friends.

One considered herself to be the leader and the other agreed. One felt less smart than the other.

These women were very vocal in expressing their feelings about comparison and I give you their words.

Sue says "I hated being compared to my twin and resented being constantly thought of as a unit of two people, rather than as an individual. It was frustrating! If my sister did something particularly good in school, I was associated with the good thing. On the negative side, if my sister did something bad, I was also associated with it. People could never seem to separate our identities and we were often referred to as 'the Johnson twins' or even 'twinnies.'

"We did receive a tremendous amount of attention all through school, which was nice in many instances. When I got into college, I had a very difficult time functioning without this built-in attention-getter."

Sue had this to say about comparison, "I remember feeling insecure about this, and I think it increased the competition between us. I felt anything I accomplished would generalize over to her, thereby taking away some of the 'glory.' Conversely, if she did something wrong, it would generalize over to me, too. I felt we were perceived as a 'unit,' rather than as two people. It wasn't until later in life, when I was alone without my twin, that I felt most insecure, because I couldn't lean on her accomplishments, her advice, her positive 'strokes' and feedback. I think my parents thought of my twin as 'the good twin,' because she didn't cause the problems I did. She always followed directions, listened to our parents, whereas I would rebel.

Ironically, I guess I rebelled partly because I wanted their attention and their *recognition* of me as an individual person who was different."

From these women's comments we see two young people yearning for their own identity; wanting to be seen for who they were—two individuals with very different personalities.

As these women reflected upon their childhood, they told me what they felt were the positive and/or negatives of being a twin as they experienced it.

They reported the positive was "the built-in ability to attract attention and instant popularity. The negative aspect being the churning, inner turmoil of competition and constant strain of trying to separate yourself from your twin—an impossible goal in the early years."

On this note Sue said, "In college my twin did well on her own, but I fared badly. I suppose, since I was the domineering twin, I was lost without my target! I felt her personality was superior to mine and her extroverted nature allowed her to meet people easier. I felt very sorry for myself after being separated from my twin."

Sally shared this, "Being a twin made my adolescent years very difficult. My twin was a real achiever, and I felt I had to keep up, yet, I really did have a different mind-set; a different personality that I wanted to explore. My twin was always correcting me, putting me down, and I think this contributed to my problems later in life with a lack of security and a need for constant praise. Even though I have sorted most of this out in therapy, the insecurity lingers. I view this lack of personal security and identity as the biggest negative that came out of my childhood as the younger twin."

Parent/Child Relationship

From a very early age it appears these twins were, as one twin put it, of a different mind-set. Early on in their development they both groped for their own identity; to be seen for who they were. One was always trying to please—the other appearing rebellious. In a sense, these twins felt they were labeled; one going one way and the other resenting being directed in the same path as her twin.

Sue, who considered herself the conservative twin, to use her words, says she resented her parents constantly looking to her for guidance of her twin sister. She says she was (privately) asked for advice in regard to her twin. While she says she is sure her parents did this unintentionally, she felt a great burden. She became firmly entrenched in her role as the "good" twin.

As Sue looks back now, she feels she missed out on the fun her twin was having. She said "I spent the greater part of my adolescent years worrying about my conduct and trying to control my sister who really was only mildly rebellious and not ever a major problem."

She wrote, "My relationship with my parents was helped because I was the 'good' twin. My parents gave me more responsibility and had higher expectations for me. This really worked against me, though, because I struggled for years trying to live up to being the eternal good girl. Looking back, it was all so unfair because my twin was never that troublesome, just full of life and the average amount of rebelliousness."

Sally wrote "My relationship with my parents was hindered because my twin was 'Goodie Two-Shoes.' My parents were always praising her good behavior, wishing I could be like her."

Both of these women sought professional help.

One considered herself the leader. Both felt jealous of the other, in competition, and inferior to the other. Both felt compared.

Wrote Sally: "My twin was the 'Mother Hen,' and I think this contributed to my problems later in life with a lack of security and a need for constant praise."

Sue: "As an adult I am very much the conformist and *still* feel burdened by my parent's high expectations of me. I still feel the favored twin and know this is not fair to my twin."

These twins were in the same classroom through grade six. They always dressed alike. One had this to say:

"We were treated as equals. It was as if we were 'one.' We felt that teachers were reluctant to favor one over the other even when the girls were aware one was more talented in one subject than the other."

They sensed the teachers saw to it that if one twin was praised for work in one area, the other twin was praised for her skills in another area. They felt they were equally liked by their teachers, but admit there were some minor seeds of jealousy between the two of them.

High school proved to be a difficult time for them. Sue clearly excelled as a student. There was jealousy on the part of her less motivated twin. Parents constantly reminded Sally she should model her behavior after her twin. This resulted in harsh feelings toward her parents. Sally felt she could never live up to the expectations of her parents, so she rebelled. She became the "party girl" while Sue studiously applied herself to the books. (Sally says it was only years later she learned her studious twin always felt jealous of her.)

Sally felt the pressure to be like Sue. The pressure she felt to conform and function like her twin sister resulted in enormous stress. As she reflects back over the years, this twin feels the pressure to conform, and the constant disapproval of her parents was the root of all her high school unhappiness.

In high school these girls were not in the same classes. Sally reports they both enjoyed comparing the different experiences they had with their teachers, and felt the teachers did not present a problem. She recognized the fact that being in different classes gave her the opportunity to feel, for the first time in her life, that she was a single entity.

It was while these girls were in separate colleges that Sally felt the feelings of insecurity and jealousy began to merge. She says "My twin had her toughest time in college, and had a difficult time adjusting to life as a 'single.' On the other hand, I had a ball, and never remember even communicating with my twin during those years."

Adult Relationship

Sue made these comments: "I think my role as the domineering twin is a role I'll always have to fight off. I tend to be authoritative, which I see as a fault growing out of twinship. I also tend to be overly critical and short on patience, both qualities being constantly honed during the twinship years. I'm crazy about my twin, but having her close by seems to rake up old problems of not being separate in others' eyes. At this point in my life I'm glad to be on my own."

Advice to Parents of Twins

Parents and teachers and society should be more aware of twins as people who are individuals, and stop saying how cute 'they' are, and where 'they' will go to college, etc.

Sue wrote, "Don't dress the twins alike. *Never* call them 'twinney' or some other double nickname. Keep them in separate classes in school and don't always give them identical presents for Christmas and birthdays. Most of all, recognize them as *two* people, rather than *one* unit. Don't ever indicate that one twin is more deserving of approval than the other twin. Don't ask one twin's advice about the other twin. Let twins enjoy twinship and recognize that twins consider themselves half of a whole. At least we felt that way.

"Don't establish a competitive atmosphere. Establish a team atmosphere, while encouraging individuality. A competitive atmosphere just leads to life-long grudges between twins, who may not be able to compete exactly alike. I believe the worst mistake my parents made was to misjudge the goodness of my twin during our teenage years when my twin was rebellious. They got into a panic about my twin because she wasn't conforming exactly to their standards. At the same time, they saw I was conforming. I think they made life hard on my twin—and that made life hard on me too. I've spent most of my life conforming and still being the 'good twin'."

Sally wrote, "Bring them up the same way you would a normal

brother and sister. Let them be their own people. Don't dress them alike. Let them each explore their own talents. Encourage them to be different. Put them in different classrooms. Celebrate their birthdays on different days. Don't compare them to each other. Praise them! Twins, more than other kids, need to be praised as individuals, to avoid a serious identity crisis later in life. Don't give them the same presents all the time. Enjoy the differences, instead of stifling them."

To give you an update on this set of twins, the twin who was married first now feels great relief that her twin is married. For many years she felt guilty that her sister was single.

Chapter Four

Looking Into the Lives of Fraternal Twins

"You can't be twins! You look nothing alike." This comment is often made to fraternal twins. Many times, as children, my twin sister and I were asked this question. Had we not been dressed alike the question would not have surfaced, since we looked no more alike than any other siblings in the family. I remember people asking me what it was like to be a twin. I never knew how to respond since being a twin was all I'd ever been. Now, when people ask this question of me I think they may be sorry they asked, for I'm sure they often learn more than they ever wanted to know.

Fraternal twins are known as two-egg twins, scientifically termed dizygotic twins. These are twins whose mother is a double ovulator and her eggs fertilized by different sperm. These twins are often known as invisible twins since they look no more alike than other siblings, and may be questioned as to whether they really are twins. On the other hand, I am often amazed at how much these twins may look alike. In fact, they may be mistaken for identical twins. They may share many or few of the same genes.

Identical/Fraternal twins are the result of one egg splitting into two equal parts before fertilization. These identical eggs are then penetrated by two different sperm.

Fraternal twins can be puzzling to new parents of twins, unless, of course, they are opposite sex twins. Fraternal twins may look more alike at birth than identical twins. As fraternals get older the differences in their physical appearance becomes much more apparent.

It's much easier to distinguish one from the other since one may have dark hair, the other blond. Their skin tone may be different. One may have inherited the large eyes of their mother, the other the smaller eyes of their father.

Most fraternals have separate placentas (however the placenta often confuses doctors since the placentas of fraternals may fuse, and the egg of identicals may divide before implantation and the halves root far apart in the womb.

Women between the ages of 35 to 39 are ten times more likely to give birth to fraternal twins than are mothers in their teens. Fraternal twins also are more likely to be borne to the mother who has given birth to several children. There is also greater likelihood of fraternal twins if there is a history of fraternal twins in the family.

Race also plays a part in bearing fraternal twins. In the United States the frequency of Orientals bearing twins is about one in 140 births. More twins are born to the black population than to any other race.

Fraternal twins are much less likely to pursue the same type of work. These twins often go their own way as adults. These twins are less likely to feel the need to live in close proximity to one another. My research has shown that fraternal women tend to nurture the twin bond more intensely than do many of the fraternal men and opposite sex twins. Yet, I hasten to add that each set of twins develops its own unique relationship.

I've included a few comments from each of the three types of these twins to give you some idea of how they felt about their lives lived as a twin.

Comments From Same-Sex Male Twins

This man in his early 40's wrote, "I left home at 18-19 for another state to escape competitiveness! To be on my own.

"Despite everyone making an issue of it, I never felt like a twin. Even dressing alike and sharing the same birthday parties neither bothered me nor brought out any special feelings whatsoever that tied me to him any more than my relationships with my other brothers.

"I have often thought about my twinship, but of all my five brothers and sisters, I am least close to my twin. I have often wished we were more similar so we would have been closer."

Another twin commented, "I honestly believe having the support of one another was the most positive attribute of our childhood. I can't think of any negative things. My twin brother and I are extremely close!"

One male twin wrote, "I like to have attention. Being a twin, especially one of three sets, is a good start for conversation with a new acquaintance."

Another twin said this: "I never felt anything positive about being a twin. My brother and I have very little in common with each other, and when we are together he doesn't have a lot to say to me. I have always felt that being his twin has created a wall between us. I might add, there are not any bad feelings between us. I love him and feel badly because we don't see more of one another.

"One negative point is that of being compared to each other. My twin was very defensive and has grown with a real temper because of being behind me in school, etc. I often felt he was picked on because of this, but never did anything to stop it.

"Since he was usually sick and was behind me in school, I really felt I was his older brother. Therefore, the negative was my being healthy while he was ailing. If he had also been in good health, we would have experienced many pleasures we were unable to enjoy."

A fraternal twin living in Hawaii wrote, "The one item that stands out as very negative about my being a twin is my dependence on my brother. I felt like I couldn't do anything without him. He was my protector. I couldn't live without him but in time this feeling drove a wedge between us. I felt resentment toward him because I couldn't function on my own. I think the turning point in my life was in my senior year in high school. I just got tired of being known as my twin's brother!"

"My parents were among only a handful of people who could tell us apart even if we are fraternal twins. Maybe that isn't a big deal, but to one being identified as someone distinct and unique from my brother, was something I cherished."

Some of these men wish they had shared more of the same interests as children and would like to have felt closer growing up, and as adults. These twins are much less likely to give thought to being a twin. These fraternals may or may not look alike, so the two of them can walk down the street together and never draw attention.

Competition between these fraternal men does not seem to be an influencing factor as adults. They have gone in different directions; for the most part they have pursued different areas of work. They do not let twinship affect the location where they want to live. Many wrote they lived great distances from their twin and do not see each other on a regular basis; however, many of them do keep in touch with their twin.

Comments From Same-Sex Fraternal Women

These fraternal women had many positive comments about being a twin. Here are a few of their statements:

"Especially in the last fifteen to twenty years I've thought a lot about my twinship. I'm not sure being a twin has affected my personal characteristics or persona as much as it has my own inner, psychological sense of self. To the extent that I idolized being a twin, I think there was a corresponding sense of shame of myself as an individual. I also identify (as the second born) with being 'hidden away.' Sometimes I experience a sense of dissatisfaction, as if a part of me is missing or I'm just not whole, and I think this robs me of a sense of fulfillment."

One fraternal woman had this to say:

"I felt inferior and dumb, and in many ways I still do.

"Some of our friends decided I wasn't old enough to be in their crowd because I was a year behind them in school, and my sister went along with them.

"I was compared with my twin when my girls were born (by my brother-in-law.) He made me feel like I was a very dumb mother but that she was perfect."

Another twin wrote,"I not only had a sister with whom I played, walked to school, or shared a room, but I also had a special friend whom I have always loved through the painful times and the good times. She is a *very special lady*, my sister.

"My sister and I were taught to look out for each other, something we still do, even though we are miles apart.

"We were given a lot of attention from outside sources: school, stores, and even the Mothers of Twins club was directed our way.

"I've thought at times how my life might have been different. I believe we often did things together at an older age because there existed a feeling that we should like similar things. There were activities neither one of us tried, probably because our roles were fairly well defined, and we stayed pretty close within those roles. This found one or the other not trying out for a sport, or even a class, because the other twin excelled in that area, and we didn't want to play one against the other. Here again, you see where comparison as well as competition enters the picture."

"Attending a different high school gave me the chance to step outside of my role and try my hand at activities I'd been hesitant to try before. It was *great*. I'm thankful I had that opportunity because it helped me visualize myself as an individual outside of my twin.

"We, you might say, built a mold of our personality out of what the other's (twin) image was or how we saw it. Therefore we may have been alike, yet we also were different.

"Play was a big part of my childhood and an important step towards my development. It began in the backyard where I first began to stand up for my twin. I learned that it proved helpful when we both worked at a project together. We learned through play that one of us might excel in one activity and not in another. We learned how to reassure one another and help build self-confidence.

"The negative aspect of being a twin for us was that we fought an awful lot. We were very competitive and for me it seems I was always competing for my mother's love, trying to be the better twin in her eyes, even though we were both equally loved."

Another twin wrote: "I believe twinship had a definite effect on my life. In my growing-up years, there was always a great deal of comparison from family, neighbors, teachers, relatives and friends.

"We were in the same classes from grade one on.

"I was labeled the 'bad' twin, since I was an extroverted tomboy type.

"My image of myself was always 'huge' since I constantly heard, 'You two can't be twins, you're so much bigger than she is.' (Two inches taller and 20 lbs. heavier.)

"Because my twin was more popular, and I felt Mom loved her best, my assumption was that quiet, introverted passive people were good and that anyone who was alive with emotion and lived life with an open honesty was bad.

"We are still exact opposites. We love and care about each other, but I feel a void because we aren't as close as I would like. Maybe it's because she is my twin that my desire to break down the barrier is so great."

Comparison is felt by all twins, but fraternal twins may be more likely to have it made toward them because there can be such a difference between them. It has been said that those who observe twins seem to look at identicals to find the differences between them and at fraternals to find any similarities.

I don't think I've known any fraternals who enjoyed being compared. Twins, just as any other person like to be seen for who they are, *themselves*.

This from a twin who was one of three twin sets in her family. "One aspect of comparison that my parents fell into with all three sets was our performance in school. This proved to be particularly hard on all of us. My twin was better at math, I had higher marks in other subjects. My twin and I always found ourselves in some form of a standoff.

"Our parents felt we should do things together since we were twins. I often had to join my twin and her friends in activities I was not interested in."

Here is a comment sent to Ann Landers from a fraternal twin, "I am a twin. When we were twelve years old I wore a size 18 dress and weighed close to 200 pounds. My twin sister wore a size eight and weighed 106 pounds. I was always 'Fatty, Fatty, two-by-four. Can't get through the kitchen door.' My twin, of course, had a great little figure.

"When Mom took us to see Dad (he was stationed at the Air Force base in Kiessler Field, MO) she asked the airline clerk for one adult fare and two children. The man behind the desk said, "Do you mean to tell me that big girl is a child?" Mom replied, "Yes, in fact, these girls happen to be twins." He looked at her and said, "That's one for Ripley's Believe It or Not." For years I had to take insults like that, not to mention the trouble I ran into buying clothes that looked good on me."

Suggestions to Parents of Twins

Over the many years of doing twin research I've had the opportunity to speak first hand with many parents of twins. Some of these parents were also twins, which I found most interesting since they had experienced life as a twin. They felt their being a twin helped them in rearing twins.

One fraternal twin, age thirty-five, says emphatically, "Treat your children as individuals. Even twins have different needs. For example, I think my twin needed more affection than I, but we got the same amount. My mother often dressed us the same when we were younger, but always in different colors. I have always appreciated the fact that we had different sounding names. It helped us be more individual."

A sixty-five-year-old says, "Most certainly do not compare them in their presence. Do not tell of their likes and dislikes. Let them be individuals. Don't make them dress alike if they do not wish to. Praise them as you would any child. Do not make one do something you would not make the other do." Her own twin adds: "Find, or take time with each one individually and let them know you love them. Maybe you don't approve of all they do, but let them know you love them for who they are." This last advice seems to be vitally important for nurturing *all* growing human beings, not just twins.

This twin expresses what many fraternal women have said, "Never, never compare. Encourage competency for each individual—in different areas in order to build confidence, not dependency."

Opposite Sex Fraternal Twins

Opposite sex fraternal twins comprise one-third of the total twin population, yet they have not shared in one-third of the attention alloted twins. The parents of these twins often feel that information and help for them are lacking. One mother had this to say, "Where are we in this mountain of research being done on twins? Nobody ever writes about the opposite sex twins."

Opposite sex fraternal twins have much to offer in the scientific research of twins. It has long been recognized that there is a difference in the rate of growth and development, both physicially, psychologically, and emotionally, between girls and boys. The differences, in and of themselves, are not what cause the problems for boys and girls, but in the case of twins, such varying differences can have a profound, and often longterm, if not life-long effect on opposite sex twins.

The damage happens when opposite sex twins are expected to perform in a similar manner due to their being the same age. These twins may both be very coordinated, may share the same interest in music, etc. but they may also not exhibit the same degree of coordination, nor share the same interest in music.

Parents of twins, and those who work with twins need to be aware of the differences between boys and girls and the degree of those differences and the rate they normally develop certain skills,etc. Boy babies, during the first year of life, tend to be heavier, as well as longer, than girls. Little girls usually develop at a faster pace prior to puberty, but are surpassed during the teen years by the spurt of growth of the male.

Since no two twins develop exactly at the same pace, it is important for parents to know each twin well, apart from their co-twin. Granting privilege to one and not the other usually asks for a show-down and has the potential for creating resentment, conflict and often hurt feelings. With twins, it is often the opposite sex twins who are most often at loggerheads with their parents over the liberties given to one and not the other.

A woman with a twin brother said, "As I look back over my childhood, nothing really stands out as being a twin. I was the dominating child. Since I was the only girl, I was able to get permission for both of us to do something easier. As we got older (eighteen to nineteen) I found it hard to understand why my brother was able to go more freely and with less hassle than I— just because I was a girl."

One advantage of having a twin of the opposite sex, wrote some of these twins, is their feeling of having an opportunity to know and experience early sharing with one of another gender. A fourteen-year-old boy wrote, "She can help me with girl problems." Twin sister shared this, "I feel more fulfilled for being a twin, especially having a brother twin as I learn both girl things and boy things."

The opportunity to have another the same age to play with was expressed by some of these opposite sex twins; however, not mentioned nearly as often as it was by the same sex twins. It was more likely to be mentioned when they were the only children in the family. Opposite sex fraternal twins born into a family where there were already boy and girl siblings gave them opportunity to relate more readily with those children who shared the same interests.

Opposite sex fraternal twins are less likely than are other twin sets to have to deal with being seen as half of a whole. They are not expected to share the same interests. Because they are twins they may be compared in a few areas, such as growth and academically, but they are spared the continuing search for personal identity, as experienced by many of the identicals.

"I believe I've been somewhat dominated by my twin, wrote the girl who has a twin brother. I think a lot of it has to do with the male/female relationship. Women's rights have not hit home in our twinship."

While the closeness of same-sex twinships may make it harder for the twins to establish relationships with members of the other gender, male-female twins may find it easier.

Of the five categories of twins, these opposite sex twins are the least likely to have problems with identity.

Here are a few of the comments made by opposite sex twins:

"We didn't look anything like brother and sister, let alone twins!"

"I'll always believe there's something special about having a twin, something out of the ordinary about it that somehow sets us apart from the ordinary crowd."

"I enjoyed being a twin because I felt special about having someone born on the same day with me."

"To me my brother was just that, a brother who was the same age as I. We were close, but I can't think of any negative or positive results. I did like saying he was my twin brother."

"I was always the larger of the two and until high school, when he became average size, I felt like a giant of some kind. Plus, I was always healthier than he."

Another comment regarding physical comparison. "I was taller and bigger and people would call me 'big, fat Sis'…but in a few years my twin brother grew really fast and was, and still is, about ten inches taller than I."

Opposite sex fraternal twins are less likely to dress alike than are same-sex twins. And parents of these twins are less likely to dress their twin children in matching outfits. The sailor style outfit was mentioned by some of these twins; however, none of these twins mentioned that they dress in coordinated outfits as adults.

One aspect of this type of twinship mentioned by many of these twins was the advantage of getting to know, at an early age, both boys and girls. "His friends were my friends, and my friends were his friends," wrote some of these twins. Some of them felt having a twin of the opposite sex made it easier for them to feel more at ease when they started to date. Because of having an opposite sex twin they felt they had been exposed to a wider variety of experiences than if they had not had a brother/sister. As one twin wrote, "I not only learned about girl's things, I also learned about what interests little boys and more about how they think and act."

Problems of sibling position are compounded by twinship. Here are some of the comments made by these opposite sex twins

"It seemed to me that my twin and I felt singled out from the family unit. As younger children, I remember feeling 'stuck in the middle,' with an older brother, 'the little man,' and the younger sister, 'baby.' My twin and I were clumped in the middle. I resented it a lot of the time."

Of all the twins dealt with in this book, it is this group of twins who most often received different toys, or gifts during their growing up years.

One male commented "Had bigger birthday parties and twice as many friends." Another wrote, "My birthday was never my own, it was always something that was shared."

This opposite sex twin set wrote, "Our Christmases and birthdays I will always remember. The other said, "The birthday parties will always be fondly remembered."

This woman wrote, "We had a party every four years. We each invited our own guests and they brought gifts only to the one that invited them. Our birthdays were not celebrated on different days. We each had our own cake."

Said this woman, "When I was a twin at home I always had to share my birthday cake with my twin brother. I was always a little jealous of other children and wanted my own. When I went off to college the girls in the dorm bought me a real nice birthday cake, and instead of being happy about it, I was sad. I missed my twin brother so much. I thought the cake tasted like sawdust and I cried later when I was by myself."

Opposite Sex Fraternal Twins and Comparison

Of the five main types of twins, it is my belief that opposite sex twins are least likely to be compared. Certainly all twins are compared to some degree but gender does appear to lessen the intensity of comparison made between twins.

"I was not only compared with my twin by my family and friends, I was also compared to my younger sister. I felt like I had 'sold' them out. I got better grades than my brother and I kept my things, clothes, etc., picked up."

"I don't recall my twin sister and I ever being compared. We grew up being very close to each other, and we are still this way. I feel very privileged to have a twin sister."

"My twin and I were so much different that when people compared us to one another it was mostly to show how different we were. We were often referred to as 'the twins,' which sometimes made me feel like I wasn't me, but one of the twins."

This woman said, "When comparisons were made (usually by teachers on our work at school), we would be annoyed. We had such different interests and aptitudes and our parents had made it clear that we were just like any brother and sister. Comparisons just didn't make sense to us."

Opposite sex fraternal twins are rarely confusing to school mates. Very often it is not known by their peers that they are twins unless they are told.

One of the biggest decisions that must be made by parents of twins regards placement of their twin children in the classroom. "Shall we let them be together, or separate them?" It's not only a very difficult and sensitive decision, but one of the most important ones that must be made. It is one that needs to be given much thought long before the children are ready to begin school.

If little children, as early as two, are given the opportunity to have brief periods away from each other, and are given early opportunity to be in the presence of other little children, they are much less likely to rebel at not being placed with their twin when they begin school.

There are positives and negatives that go with them being together, as well as being separated. The responses from these opposite sex twins were both for and against. They felt it less crucial that opposite sex twins be separated than those of same-sex twins. Yet, the overall feeling was that it is probably best for them to be in separate classrooms.

The comments made by these twins indicated they did not spend as much time with their twin while in school as did same sex twins. They often walked home together, several of them mentioning they, especially the girls, felt added protection because of having their twin with them.

One man wrote,"I want to say my twin was the smart one in school. But of all the flak I received was not so much from my family but from the school teachers, from grade one to twelve. When I didn't do something up to standard, they would always say, 'but look how well Mary did it.' On looking back, it's a wonder I didn't get a complex of some type, but I always just took her for granted, as she *never* said anything."

A woman twin said, "I hated having to compete and be compared with my twin, instead of being looked at as self-confident. If I hadn't been so compared with him, I think I'd be more outgoing. I try very hard to be sweet and nice to everybody and not to hurt anyone.

Some of these opposite sex twins feel they are closer as adults than they were as children. Others feel they have grown apart as they have grown older. As these adult twins reflected back over their lives some of them wished they had not been so domineering and bossy with their twin; others wished they had shared more activities with their twin.

As children some of the girls took on a protective and sometimes dominating attitude toward their twin. As adults they have told me they regret their dominant demeanor over their twin as children. I've also observed the male twin who maintained a dominant role over the twin sister. Being parents to twins is not always an easy one. It is important, however, to be aware of the control one twin is having over the life of the other twin.

All parents want their children to enjoy one another as adults. Our gift of memory sometimes makes it difficult to not let the actions of the past color our feelings as we grow older. It is important, however, to try to forgive seemingly unfair treatment dealt you as children, and to enjoy the happy moments you recall and anticipate with your twin.

My study shows there is much less parallelling of lives between the opposite sexes compared with the lives of many of the identical twins. Twins whose lives parallel each other are most likely to be in very close touch with their twin throughout life. It very often happens that the opposite sex twins find they have a closer bond later on in life rather than during the early period of their life.

If the girl in the twin set is a tomboy, then it is more likely the two of them will spend more time together. If the girl is very feminine there is the greater chance she will identify more readily with the activities of the mother, or of other girl siblings. The boy will spend more time with other boyfriends or with brothers in the family.

One twin made this comment about the adult relationship:"As you get older, being a twin becomes more special.

"I have always enjoyed being a twin, and often volunteer this information. Our lives have been very different and for many years we were not close, but as time has gone on we have become very close.

"On an occasion or two my twin has been known to make a decision for me because she's my twin. I have to tell you this has sometimes had difficult results, but I'm so touched by her strong feelings for me (mutual!) that it's more 'sweet' than annoying."

Twins and parents of twins often send me poems. In the book you'll notice I've included a few of them. Here's one written by a woman who gave birth to three sets of twins. And to think she had time to write poetry!

Poem written by Coletta Rempe for Jack and JoAnn

Our family was growing
By leaps and bounds
Four children, all girls
Were making the rounds

When suddenly way up there
Way out in the blue
Two more kids were heard yelling
To come down here too.

"Ok," said God. "I'll send you
with joy
But just to be different
One girl and a boy.

"I'll make the girl pretty
She'll stand straight and tall
The boy will be terrific
When handling a ball.

"I'll make them so happy
So carefree and gay
The Rempe's will love them
It's needless to say.

"So Greeting, my Jo Jo,
Happy Birthday, Jack, too.
Best wishes and good things
From the Rempes to You.

Chapter Five

Fraternal Men

Bill and Pat

One older brother and sister. Bill married an identical twin and they have boy/girl twins.

Childhood

Bill and his twin attended nursery school. They were in the same classroom in the third and fifth grade and in classes together through the twelfth grade. Bill recalls being dressed alike when small but did not choose to dress alike when older. Bill says he was often jealous of his twin. He did not consider himself the leader. He often felt he was in competition with his twin. He did not feel inferior or consider himself to be less attractive than his twin. He did not feel dominated by his twin. He did feel he was often compared to his twin. He made these comments about comparison: "It is hard as a twin and as a parent of twins not to compare twins. I was fortunate in that my parents allowed my brother and me to go our separate ways."

Pat was firstborn. He also recalls being dressed alike when small but chose not to dress alike when older. He said he was not jealous of his twin. He did consider himself to be the leader. He often felt he was not as smart as his twin. He didn't feel inferior, nor did he feel less attractive than his twin. He did not feel dominated by his twin. They shared the same bedroom until they were fourteen years old.

He felt he and his twin were often compared and made these comments about comparison. "Seems like twins are *always* compared by everyone. But it didn't make much difference to me. I always felt pretty self-assured and our parents built our self-esteem from a young age."

Pat had this to say as he reflected upon his childhood as a twin. "Bill and I were pretty good friends through most of our childhood. This provided a good amount of emotional security. We also learned a lot from each other."

Parent/Child Relationship

Bill did not feel either parent showed favoritism, nor did he feel his performance was compared with his twin. He was encouraged to develop his own extracurricular activities. This was his comment as he reflected back upon his relationship with his parents: "The fact that my parents were fair and supportive was a good foundation for my development."

Pat felt his parents never showed favoritism. He did feel his performance was compared with that of his brother. He made this comment about his relationship with his parents: "Our parents tried to be incredibly fair and treated us as individuals, mostly because we were quite different in many ways."

Adult Relationship

Bill enjoys being with his twin and feels no competitiveness with his brother. He feels he has a closer relationship with his brother than with his other siblings.

As Bill reflected back upon his twinship he said, "In our early years, the constant companionship gave us a feeling of security with our world. But with our separate ways of life in recent years our 'twinship' seems more a novelty than anything else."

Pat also enjoys being with his twin and feels the closeness has become greater as he has grown older. He feels no competitiveness with his twin. He also feels closer to his twin brother than to other siblings. As Pat reflected back upon life lived as a twin he said, "It's been beneficial overall. Because our personalities were so different in many ways I feel I had a better indoctrination in human nature while growing up—hence I'm a good 'people' person. I understand human nature well."

Advice to Parents of Twins

Bill offers this to parents of twins, "Allow them to seek their own paths in life."

Pat advises, "Be fair. Recognize that all children are different regarding talents, skills, likes, dislikes, etc. Keeping this in mind, it's easier to help build children's self-esteem, which is extremely important, especially with twins."

Tony and Sam

I chose this set of twins to show that some fraternal twins can look very much alike. They are definitely fraternal, or two-egg twins, but are most often mistaken for one another. This set of twins has younger brothers.

Childhood

The responses to all childhood questions were the same. These young men who were eighteen when they completed the questionnaire recalled they were sometimes dressed alike as children but when older did not choose to accentuate their look-alike appearance. They shared some classes in school until the sixth grade. Neither felt he was the leader. They did not feel that one was smarter, inferior or less attractive than the other. They did feel competitive with one another.

Tony had this to say about comparison: "Personally I did not mind any comparison made between my twin and me. We were either considered one unit or we were considered so individual that comparisons made would be akin to comparing apples and oranges. To my mind, any comparison would be a compliment to me. I still often think of us as one unit, though I know we are two very different people."

Sam made these comments regarding comparison: "I was often annoyed when I was compared to my brother because I thought the comparisons were unjustified. We were, and still are, two different individuals."

Childhood

Tony had this to say upon reflection of his childhood: "I guess my wanting to be viewed as someone completely different than my brother forced me to become more independent, but I kind of doubt it. I suppose I became more competitive academically because of him."

Sam responded by saying, "As a result of being a twin, one has the distinct advantage of having your own brother as your own peer. So if one did not know how to act or what to do in a given situation you could ask your twin without any degree of guilt or embarrassment. A distinct disadvantage was that even though we were fraternal twins, we were often seen as one social/economic/political entity. We were never Tony and Sam, but the Johnson boys, or the Johnson brothers, or the Johnson twins. It seemed it was easier for people to at first ignore our individual characters and deal with us as a unit. However, as they got to know us, they treated us more as individuals."

Parent/Child Relationship

These twins did not feel favoritism was ever shown by either parent. One of them felt his performance was compared with his brother. Both appreciated their parents encouraging them in their own desires regarding extracurricular activities.

Tony said this as he reflected back on the parent/child relationship: "When we were younger, we were encouraged to dress alike, adopt similar interests and always be exactly alike. I have a notion this was done merely out of convenience and not out of some perverse cruelty. It was merely easier for my mother, being a first-time mother, to deal with one entity (a set of twins who appeared identical to each other) rather than two very different entities. As we grew older and less alike, my mother and father realized we should be allowed to develop our own identities. We have developed separate interests and different abilities, but we're still alike in many ways and even share the same group of friends."

Sam commented, "My parents were among only a handful of people who could tell us apart, even if we were fraternal twins. Maybe that isn't a big deal, but to one being identified as someone distinct and unique from my brother, was something I cherished."

Adult Relationship

Both of these men, as adults, enjoy being with one another and they feel their degree of closeness has increased over the years. One of them remarked he still has some feelings of competitiveness with his twin. Both feel closer to one another than to their younger siblings.

Tony made these comments as he reflected on his adult relationship with his brother and the effects twinship has possibly had on his life: "I don't believe twinship has had much effect on my life. It was only in our childhood that we were treated as identical to one another, therefore having the same interests. Later we were encouraged to develop our own individualities."

Tony went on to say he does feel twinship has played a part in how his personality is today. "Sometimes you think of yourself and your twin as one unit. His abilities and interests sort of become yours. So, in effect, I've developed a very complimentary personality with my twin. That is, our personalities are not identical. In fact they could be regarded as opposites, but somehow our personalities complement each other."

Sam shared this, "I've always felt my unique bond with my twin brother has made me more knowledgeable about the motives and actions of others. This is due to my deep understanding of my twin's behavior and his understanding of mine. Our relationship has made us somewhat introverted, for we enjoy talking amongst ourselves about esoteric topics instead of talking to others in a more somber state of conversation."

Advice to Parents of Twins

This is the advice Tony offers to parents of twins: "I can't speak for identical twins, but for fraternal twins, you can raise them as two different brothers who just happened to be the same age. Even though fraternals share many things in common, they can be very different people."

He goes on to say, "It is good to put them in their own unique environment, i.e. separating once in a while to see what they like themselves, without their twin. The more time twins spend together, the more alike and dependent they become."

Sam offered this advice, "Dress them differently! Treat them as individuals and not as a single entity."

Rod and Mike

This set of twins comes from a family of three sets of twins and a younger brother.

Childhood

Mike was firstborn. They shared a lot of the same playmates. These twins attended the same school and were in the same classroom. He recalls being dressed alike as small children but did not choose to dress alike when older. He did not feel jealous of his twin, nor did he consider himself the leader. He did feel he was not as smart as his twin, often felt inferior to him and usually felt in competition with him. He did not feel dominated by his twin. He did feel he was often compared with his twin by family and friends.

Mike wrote this about being compared. "I felt inferior to him in terms of intelligence. He always did better in his studies than I. Our report cards were always compared and I often wondered after we were out of school if I just quit trying because he was better at book studying. I knew he would get the assignments for the following days class so I just wouldn't bother with it. As far as attractiveness, I was much larger than he and was often told I was handsome. He was quite a lot smaller than I, and was always having to prove himself, certainly not to me but to himself. He was very high-strung and I am easygoing. My father considered me lazy, and maybe I was."

Rod was second born. He was not jealous of his twin, often considered himself the leader, usually felt inferior and less attractive than his twin. He did not feel dominated by his twin.

He often felt he was compared with his twin by both family members and friends. He had this to say about comparison.

"Twins are *always* compared by everyone. One is faster, smarter, more lazy, taller, heavier, stronger, better looking, etc. Most people, including my parents, were wrong in their conclusion on *some* comparisons."

Parent/Child Relationship

Mike shared this, "I feel my parents showed more favoritism toward me. I also feel they compared our performance. I do feel that punishment was administered fairly. I don't feel our parents encouraged me to develop my own extracurricular activities.

"My parents showed favoritism toward me for several reasons. Since I made better grades in school they thought I was more intelligent. (Not so!) I was hyperactive, in their opinion, and my twin was much less active so he was labeled as lazy (not so!). He did my work lots of times. Because he was very stubborn he got more punishment than I, at the times when we were all punished at once. He took a lot of abuse from me because he was good-natured and I was aggressive."

Rod wrote, "I felt that favoritism was shown my twin. I felt that I was very often compared with my brother. I was given a derogatory nickname by one of my parents." He did not elaborate further about his relationship with his parents.

Adult Relationship

Mike wrote, "On the positive side I'd say my twin and I could share with each other things we shared with no one else, ever. Still do! Out of the three sets of twins in our family, my twin and I were the closest and most compatible. There was less competition between us. He is more aggressive, much bigger, stronger, sensitive, understanding, and more tolerant of me than I of him."

Rod wrote, "The positive side of being a twin was that I was never lonely for lack of a friend. I felt I was very close to my twin. The negative is that I never had to make friends because of my twin and other brothers; therefore I still do not have but a couple of what I call close friends."

Mike wrote, "I feel I am very generous and sharing because of growing up that close to someone. Since we never did look like twins or hardly even like brothers, we didn't have the same kinds of experiences as a lot of twins. Most of the time when we told somebody we were twins, we had to go on to prove it if we could."

Rod shared this, "Since our first names and middle initials are very similar in look, we got our shot records and pay records mixed up in the Army. We were drafted at the same time."

Mike reported he enjoys being with his twin and his closeness with him has become greater as he has gotten older. He feels he has a closer relationship with his twin than with other siblings. He added, "Being a twin in our family was not as unique as being a single. Since our family was large, sharing was the name of the game."

Rod stated he enjoys being with his twin but the closeness had not increased over the years. He no longer feels competitive toward his twin.

Advice to Parents of Twins

Mike offers this advice, "It's probably the easy thing to give advice to parents, but to follow through with it has to be hard. You could say, do not compare them. Look at them as individuals and separate them as much as possible. That has to be hard to do when they are born together and sleep together."

Rod said, "Let them be individuals. Separate them in school if possible. Judge them independently of each other. Get to know one of them at a time."

Jay and Ken

One older brother and one younger sister

Childhood

Jay was firstborn. He shared classes with his brother until the 8th grade. He recalls not sharing a lot of the same playmates. Jay remembers being dressed the same as his brother. He was not jealous of his twin, nor did he think of himself as leader. He was never mistaken for his twin. He did not feel inferior to his twin but often thought of himself as being less attractive than his brother. He did not feel dominated by his twin. Jay recalls being compared with his twin by family and friends. He says this regarding comparison: "For the most part it was OK to discuss who was better at what. We were equally as good at something but they were usually different things. Schooling abilities were usually equal (GPA). We were both 'artsy'—him in a graphical sense and I in a more mechanical sense. I was never offended by family comparisons. I had no anxieties or ill feelings for my brother or the people doing the comparing. Honestly, he was my brother like my other brothers—not my twin."

As Jay reflected back upon his childhood he said, "Despite everyone making an issue of it, I never felt like a twin. Even dressing alike and sharing the same birthday parties did not bother me, or bring out any special feelings whatever that tied me to him any more than my relationships with my other brothers."

Ken also remembered not sharing a lot of the same playmates. He recalls being dressed alike when small but not electing to when older. He remembers being given the same toys, and birthdays always being shared with his twin brother. He did not feel jealous of his twin, nor did he feel inferior or less attractive than his twin. He did not feel dominated by his twin. Ken did feel he was sometimes compared with his twin by family members and friends, but did not elaborate.

He did say he and his twin took turns being the leader—it all depending upon which one had the best idea at the time.

Parent/Child Relationship

Jay felt his parents showed no favoritism toward him or his brother. He felt punishment was given fairly to each of them. He said he was encouraged to take part in activities that were of interest to him.

Ken shared this about his relationship with his parents: "We were a complete family until my preteen years. My father drank heavily and was very hard on my mother. At times he severely beat her. That's what caused and resulted in the divorce. My twin brother and I shared the same large room with beds about 25' apart. My bed was close to the stairs leading up to the living room and the door at the top was always closed at night. Many nights I would wake to hear my father being cross with my mother. I often heard sounds that indicated to me he was even beating her. I'm sure it was usually a belt or his hands, since I know the belt was personally used on me for my own punishment. I'm sure he was more kind to me with it than he was to my mother. The next morning my mother would be quiet, pouting, but somberly normal to us as she got us off to school. She showed no outward signs of the night before except bad bruises on her face and arms. No questions were asked and no explanations given.

"Despite all of this I never had feelings of hatred for my father doing this to my mom. I never thought about whether my mother deserved it. It just happened. Their fights started outside their relationship with us and that's where we left it. I'm not sure if I ever loved my father, but I respected him. My mother did well with us on her own. She was strong enough to discipline us but not overshadow us. We all have good careers and none of us are in any trouble. I can't complain."

Ken also said he felt no favoritism was shown them by either parent. He did say his parents compared his school work with that of his twin on occasion. He made these two comments regarding parent/child relationship:"We always had the same room together when we lived in a house that had limited bedrooms. It was always assumed by our parents that we should be together in the same room."

Advice to Parents of Twins

This is the advice Jay offers to parents of twins: "Don't try to treat them the same. No matter what, they are individuals. Don't exploit the fact that they are twins in order to draw attention to a natural phenomenon. Don't compare them or expect them to do the same things. If you can help it, don't even dress them alike."

Ken had this to offer: "Treat them as individuals, not expecting them to do the same things or act the same way."

Lonnie and Gary

Three sets of twins in this family and three singleton siblings.

Lonnie, the firstborn, recalls being dressed alike as a small child but did not choose to dress alike when older. He was not jealous of his twin nor did he feel competitive with his twin. He did consider himself the leader. He did not feel less smart than his twin, nor inferior or less attractive. He did not feel dominated by his twin. These twins were in the same classroom until the third grade.

Gary also recalls being dressed alike when small, but chose not to dress alike when older. He felt jealous of his twin, felt less smart, and felt in competition with his twin. He did not consider himself the leader, nor did he feel he was dominated by his twin. He did not feel inferior to his twin, nor less attractive. He did feel comparison was made by family members and friends.

Lonnie did feel he was compared by family members and friends. These were his comments: "My twin and I got along quite well and did not compete until my twin was held back in the third grade. This started a lot of problems. Our friends were chosen apart, and my twin was put down for not being as smart as his brother, etc. We also competed athletically, in which I excelled until in high school."

Gary made this comment regarding comparison, "I didn't like it at all. I feel that it hurt during my growth period."

Childhood

Lonnie said, "We grew up doing everything together. We seemed to be much more independent, not dependent on our parents so much. We had each other to play with when no one was around. We could discuss problems, experiences and questions we each had. One negative point is that of being compared to each other. My twin was very defensive and has grown with a real temper because of being behind me in school. I often felt he was picked on because of this, but never did anything to stop it."

Gary wrote, "I never had to be alone. I always had someone to talk to. When the two of us do something together I am generally a little more forward or outspoken. In sports, I am very protective. I'm the bigger of the two."

Parent/Child Relationship

Lonnie says there were times when he felt his parents showed favoritism toward him, and times when he felt his parents favored his twin. He feels his parents compared him with the performance of his brother. He feels that punishment was fair for him and his twin brother.

"Because we had such a large family, both of my parents worked much of my childhood. At times my dad was gone for months. My oldest sister raised my brother and me most of our lives. But this wasn't bad, my mother took us camping. She read stories to us every night. My dad was our scout leader, took us fishing, hunting, etc. Even though there was an absence of parents often, I have grown up loving them and respecting them for what they have accomplished. They showed favoritism towards certain kids at times, but each got his turn and we all grew up levelheaded and we are a very close family."

Gary did not feel favoritism was shown him, but sensed his father did show favoritism to his brother. He felt punishment was given fairly. He said he was encouraged to pursue activities of his choice. My father and I never got along, which made it that much harder on my mother."

Lonnie wrote, "My twin has a very stubborn personality. I don't like being stubborn. I have watched his temper and stubbornness take him from job to job, lose good friends, etc. Being a twin has helped me not be afraid to show affection and love for people.

Adult Relationship

Lonnie said, "I enjoy being a twin and I have grown with this feeling which is stronger as I get older. I enjoy being with my twin and do not feel any competitiveness toward him. I do not feel closer to my twin than I do to other siblings in my family. I think I have experienced many things that other people (non-twins) haven't. I can't imagine being an only child. It has made me understand why people act the way they do since I've been with another person so long.

"What stands out now is that any time we need support, advice, or just someone to shoot the breeze with we always call each other. We know the other will drop anything and listen fully to what we say, and best of all, will give a truthful feeling back. This confidence in each other helps one in many situations. Two heads are better than one."

Gary wrote, "I enjoy being with my twin; however, I do not feel the twin bond has become greater with the years. I still feel some competitiveness toward my twin. I do not feel I have a closer relationship with my twin than with other siblings."

Advice to Parents of Twins

Lonnie shared this, "I think they should try to help each child individually with his interests, not just the interest of the most outspoken. Also, don't compare them on everything—grades, sports, manners, etc. I think my brother and I had a lot of problems because of the saying, 'Why can't you be like your brother.' Treat them not only as twins but also individuals."

Gary said this, "Treat them as individuals."

Author's note: Lonnie wrote what I'm sure many of the twins who took part in the research thought when he wrote, "It's tough to sit down and write about this. I've been a twin for 24 years and really never thought about how twinship has affected me. I'm very interested in the results."

Chapter Six

Fraternal Women

Kay and Donna

A sister one year older and a sister eight years younger.

These girls always attended the same schools and shared most of their classes. They were dressed alike when small and throughout most of their school years chose to dress alike. They were given similar gifts, and their birthdays were always celebrated together.

Kay sometimes felt jealous of her twin, felt in competition with her twin and felt less smart. She felt inferior to her twin. She knew keenly the sting of comparison. These are her words: "Comparison was hard. My twin was always stronger willed. I was more attractive, so we were always compared—even today! You never get away from it. We live in separate cities, so people don't even know I have a twin—same with her." This twin says she often felt dominated by her twin.

Donna did not see herself as the leader twin. She did feel she was less attractive than her twin and added, "If you saw us now you would think we were not of the same family!" She did not feel dominated by her twin but added, "My twin said I did

dominate her." Donna was not jealous of her twin, did not feel
less smart, nor did she feel inferior.

About comparison, Donna wrote, "Because we were very
different people, I would like to think we were our own selves.
We may have had the same friends, but they liked us for who we
were. My twin was very quiet and I guess I was loud."

Childhood

Kay stated they were often mistaken for one another, yet they
looked nothing alike. She told me, "My twin had straight hair,
mine was curly. She always had acne; I didn't. She was always
heavier than I—even today."

As Kay reflected on her childhood, she wrote, "I liked being
a twin. In fact, I was hoping I would have a set of twins. You
always have a friend to talk to or be with. She and I are very
close. The only bad thing about being a twin is that you're always
compared. But my two daughters who are three years apart feel
the same way. I think it's natural to compare children, whether
they are twins or not."

Donna said, "I always had a friend! Sad or happy! To be a
twin is the greatest thing that could happen to anyone. I'm glad it
happened to me. She is my best friend! And I love her dearly. I
would do anything for her and I know she would do the same.
We both help each other in our lives (children, husband's business,
family.) We are very lucky to have each other.

Parent / Child Relationship

Since this set of twins had a sister one year older they were
often perceived as triplets, and often dressed alike. Kay wrote,
"Our older sister was our parents' favorite. We two did everything
wrong, our older sister always seemed to be right. I often fought
with her—I never did with my twin. When we were teenagers
my parents bought one car. The three of us had to share it, and
we always had to go together! So our older sister was either stuck
with us or we were stuck with her. I think that was our parents'

biggest mistake. We could never go out without each other."

Donna felt favoritism was shown her older sister. She commented, "I honestly feel our parents were fair with both of us. My twin and I were close most of the time and we still are. When I need help I can call her for anything.

"I remember when I moved a long distance from her. My twin went into the hospital for a week because of a slight mental breakdown. She wanted me to come and I couldn't at that time. From what I understand, my parents said it was because I left the area. It's hard to say if that's true. My twin was having problems with her job and her boyfriend at the time. But you see this was the first time we had ever been apart. We always took care of each other."

Adult Relationship

Kay enjoys being with her twin. She does feel she sometimes compares the performances of her children and her twin's children. She also feels she has a closer relationship with her twin than with her other siblings.

Donna says emphatically she always enjoys being with her twin. She does not feel she compares the performances of her children and her twin's children. She feels she knows her twin very well.

Here is what she says about being a twin. "I have never felt alone. I could always call her if I had something that was bothering me. My twin will always be there for me! And I for her! One time my twin was having problems with her husband and called me to see if I would go to another state to see our parents. I took time off from work to go with her. By being a twin, I believe I have learned more in giving, understand, caring, helping, laughing and enjoying."

Reflections on Twinship

Kay said, "My twin was always stronger than I. I usually did what she said. I was the good girl and she was, I guess, the bad. It took until I was married and had children of my own to have a stronger personality. I never gave my opinion until I was married. Now you can't shut me up. I always cared a great deal about my appearance, my twin didn't. Our personalities were different but I usually did what she said. I was weaker, but not anymore. My twin always looked after me in school. She would get very mad at someone if they hurt me. I guess she felt I couldn't take care of myself. My twin was always tough. I was her pretty twin.

Advice to Parents

Kay says, "Let them be themselves! Don't make them do the same things. They are two people, not *one*."

Donna offers this advice. "Treat both children as if they were not twins. They are two people. Don't treat them the same! Don't compare!"

Kathy and Sharon

This set of twins has one older sister and one younger brother.

Childhood

These twins were in the same classes until Junior High. They shared a lot of the same playmates, recall being dressed alike when small and often chose to dress alike as they got older.

Kathy did feel she was in competition with her twin and felt less smart. This twin did not consider herself to be the leader. She felt inferior to her twin, considered herself less attractive than her twin and felt she was compared with her twin. About comparison she wrote, "We were both good in different things. We had different outstanding qualities, so things evened out. We were compared in good taste."

Sharon was not jealous of her twin. She did consider herself to be the leader. Like her twin sister, she also felt inferior to her twin, also less attractive than her twin. She also felt compared with her twin. About comparison she wrote, "I did not feel I was compared by family, but friends were terrible about comparing us. They were often jealous of our togetherness and comparison causes trouble. Children often tried to come between us. We laugh about it now. Now it doesn't matter." Sharon did not feel dominated by her twin. Kathy felt she was often dominated.

As Kathy reflected upon childhood she made these comments: "I always had someone there to listen and be with. I could always count on her, always, even now. We've always been told we were identical but I have dark, dark brown eyes and she has light brown eyes. How can we find out what we are?" (I have helped her become informed in this regard.)

"We've never really known if we are identical or fraternal," wrote both of these women. The doctor said they were identical because there was one sack and placenta. *Author's note:* These women had different blood types, so we know they are not identical. One is Rh negative, the other Rh positive.

As Sharon reflects back upon her childhood she writes, "The positive was never being alone. To this day I hate being alone. That is probably why I have four children. My twin is still my best friend."

Parent/Child Relationship

Kathy's answers to all questions regarding the relationship with her parents were positive. She did say they were not encouraged to develop their own extracurricular activities. She made this comment, "I think our parents did a wonderful job raising us with love and attention shared equally."

Sharon did not feel favored over her twin sister. She did not feel comparison from her parents. She had this to say, "Our folks were in their middle thirties when they had us. They were excited about twins after so many years of having no more children. I do feel they were disappointed we were not boys. Or a boy and girl. They did finally get their son, three-and-one-half years later. He was more important a milestone to the family than we twins had been. Sons are really still a big issue in most families. I know. I had two daughters ten years before I had two sons."

Adult Relationship

Today Kathy very much enjoys being with her twin and her affection for her becomes even greater as they have grown older. She has never felt she compared the performance of her children with that of her twin sister's children.

Sharon enjoys being with her twin and the closeness has increased over the years. She feels she has a closer bond with her twin than with other siblings. Here are her comments about twinship, "I am not very independent because I was never alone in making a decision. I like the closeness of being with only one person at a time. I am very family minded. I do think I make judgements based on the view of 'our' thinking, not 'my' thinking. I don't know if it is good or bad, but I think we are all products of our family home and childhood. I feel I'm open and maybe too trusting of all people and situations. Particularly due to the fact that I could do no real wrong in the eyes of my twin sister. I wouldn't do it over again alone for anything. I am proud to have her at my side. Twins are great people. We don't need anyone else."

Kathy wrote, "We are very close, but I really think brothers or sisters can be just as close as twins. My twin and I grew up wanting to be together, but I was very close to my younger brother.

Our older sister is sixteen years older and we hardly knew her."

Sharon says, "We were married a year apart at the ages of seventeen and eighteen. We were both divorced a year apart at twenty-six and twenty-seven. I have four children: two girls and two boys. My twin has one boy. She lost one boy and two girls through miscarriage. We both drive Ford Broncos. We live two blocks apart. We have the same political views, same religious views and the same hang-ups."

Sharon said, "It's fun to have people ask, 'Which one are you?' When we were little our girl friends always tried to get us to hate each other, but it never worked. We think they were jealous they weren't a twin."

Advice to Parents of Twins

Kathy advises parents of twins to let them grow at their own pace. "One may be slower but often catches up and succeeds in his or her own way."

Sharon says, "Let them be one or two as the mood depends. Relax and let them enjoy each other. They are special. Give them the support they need. Separation comes naturally with schools, friends, marriages and the hustle and bustle of everyday life."

Debbie and Lisa

These twins had one older brother and three older sisters.

Childhood

These twins attended the same school and were in the same classes throughout most of their school years. Debbie recalls being dressed alike as small children but chose to dress differently when older. She did not feel in competition with her twin. She felt she as smart as her twin. She did not feel inferior nor less attractive than her twin. Debbie did not feel dominated by her twin. She did sense she was compared by family members and friends. She wrote this about comparison: "I did not like being compared at all!! Although I imagine it is inevitable when one is a twin. People seemed to expect us to be alike just because we were twins. In fact we were very different in most respects."

Lisa was firstborn. Growing up she felt jealous of her twin. She did consider herself the leader. She felt in competition with her twin. She did not feel less smart. This twin felt inferior to her twin, also felt less attractive and felt she was compared by family members and friends. She did not feel dominated by her twin. They shared the same bedroom and the same bed.

Debbie made these comments as she reflected back upon her life lived as a twin. "It was nice to have a twin since she was my very own age and we played together and shared together. I felt very close to my twin as a child, but grew apart as we got older. It seemed she was often naughty and doing something wrong and I usually felt very sorry for her. I remember her often telling me I was dumb and putting me down. In fact, it wasn't until we graduated from high school and I went to Business School and made the Honor Roll that I realized I wasn't so stupid."

In sharing thoughts on comparison Lisa wrote, "In my growing up years there was always a great deal of comparison from family, neighbors, teachers, relatives and friends. We lived in a small town and were in the same classes from first grade on. I was labeled the 'bad' twin, being an extroverted tomboy type, while my twin was nice, sweet and introverted." Also my image of myself was always 'big' since I constantly heard, 'you two can't be twins, you're so much bigger than she is' (2" taller and 20 pounds heavier.)

Parent / Child Relationship

Debbie states she did not feel her parents showed favoritism toward her or her twin. She did feel she was compared with her twin. She felt her father did not punish them fairly.

Lisa did not feel her parents showed favoritism for her but

rather for her twin. She felt her parents pitted her performance against that of her twin. She says she was given a derogatory nickname by her parents. She does not feel punishment was dealt fairly. She also felt she was not encouraged to participate in extracurricular activities that did not include her twin.

As Debbie reflected back upon her parent/child relationship she wrote, "I thought my mother was great and such a selfless person, and I loved her very much. She gave her *all* to her children. My father was the disciplinarian, very mean and nasty. I often thought he was crazy and had many negative thoughts about him. I was afraid of him. In spite of this, I can remember many times spent doing fun things (his taking us to the museum, parks, for walks, movies, etc.) and I felt he did love us. He was constantly preaching or lecturing and always expected perfection. I think having a twin to vent some of my anger probably was very helpful to me."

Lisa wrote, "Because my twin was more popular I felt Mom loved her best. My assumption was that quiet, introverted, passive people were good, and anyone who was alive with emotion and lived life with open honesty was bad.

"After many years of therapy I sorted through all the garbage and have felt very good about myself and my life for some time."

Adult Relationship

Debbie says she usually enjoys being with her twin but the closeness has not become greater as they have grown older. She doesn't feel closer to her twin than she does to her other siblings.

Debbie states, "I have never dwelt on my twinship and only sound off when someone asks 'How did you like being a twin?' It has a definite effect on one's life. Some good, some bad. In my childhood, I believe I felt more secure at times because I had a twin, even though at times she put me down."

Lisa said "My twin and I are still exact opposites. We love and care about each other. And we always have a wonderful time when we visit but I feel a void because we aren't as close as I would like. I am closer to three other sisters (and they to me) than I am to my twin. Maybe it is because she is my twin that my desire to break down the barrier is so great."

Advice to Parents of Twins

A short sentence covers it all for Debbie. She advises, "Do not compare!" She goes on to say, "I think people have a tendency to 'label' twins (especially fraternal), 'the prettier, 'the smarter', 'the noisier', 'the quieter', whatever. Consequently one twin is always feeling good, the other bad, depending on the comment and how her feelings are about herself. We, I would say, were labeled 'good' and 'bad' as children. I probably fared better since I was 'good'. I have been able to look back and see how damaging it was on my twin."

Lisa says, "Treat each as an individual and not as a team. Make no comparisons and relate to each as though the other person didn't exist."

Jane and Linda

The family of this set of twins consisted of fourteen siblings. To date only eleven are alive. Three sets of twins were born into this family.

Childhood

Jane recalls sharing the same classroom with her twin from kindergarten through the seventh or eighth grade. They were dressed alike as small children but chose not to dress alike when they were older. They were always given similar toys. She did not feel jealous of her twin and did not consider herself the leader. She was never mistaken for her twin, did not feel less smart or inferior to her twin. She did feel she was compared by family members and friends. She had this to say about comparison. "One aspect of comparison my parents fell into with all three sets was our performance in school. This proved to be particularly hard on all of us.

"Math, a subject which always seemed to come easier for my twin is a good example. I can remember no matter how hard I tried, I never achieved the same grade. A lot of long hours and tears went into my math work, but it didn't seem to help. My parents would remind my twin of all the time I spent on homework and all the free time she seemed to have. I would remind them that I enjoyed most of my studies and therefore might spend more time on them. This never seemed to appease them and my twin and I always found ourselves in some form of a standoff.

"Another phase of comparison which people used was a form of logic. If stated it would have read as such: since they are twins they must like doing the same things. I remember a dance in the tenth grade my twin and some of her friends wanted to attend. My parents told my twin 'no,' unless I'd go. I didn't want to, even though they thought I would. It ended up I went, after much peer pressure and twin pressure, too. Sometimes it was easier to go along."

Linda stated that she was often jealous of her twin. She considered herself the leader, and did not usually feel she was in competition with her twin. She did not feel less smart than her twin, inferior to her twin, nor less attractive.

About being compared, Linda did feel she was somewhat compared by family members and friends. She wrote, "We were always pitted against each other as kids. I was the radical child, my parents thought. I was often told, 'Why can't you be like your sister, and do this or that like your sister does?'

"Yes, sometimes I did feel dominated by my twin."

As Linda reflected on her childhood, she wrote, "We were always expected to do everything together. If one didn't, then neither did. On the positive side, there was always someone there who understood, perhaps not so much understood but someone who would at least listen."

Parent/Child Relationship

Jane felt no favoritism was shown by either parent. She does feel her parents often compared them. She feels they could have encouraged them to pursue their own interests.

Linda shares this, "Mom and Dad were very good parents in most ways. I did not feel they showed favoritism, but we did live next door to my grandmother most of our younger years. I felt that she showed favoritism toward my twin.

"My parents always called me a tomboy, which was true most of the time, and still is true."

Jane writes, "I had not only a sister with whom I played, walked to school, or shared a room. I also had a special friend whom I have always loved through the painful times and the good times. She is a *very special lady,* my twin sister.

"The positive outweighs the negatives of twinship. This is not to say we never had spats. We did, and usually over silly things such as, her side of the room being messy, my wanting the light on, one of us wanting to dress alike while the other one didn't, etc. But somehow we worked through them and they helped us build a better friendship."

"We were taught by our mother to always watch out for each other. I'm thankful for that advice and even today we still tend to 'look out' for each other even though we are many miles apart. I have seen my twin brothers and sisters also follow this advice and it has proven to be very positive.

Adult Relationship

Jane says she usually enjoys being with her twin and the relationship has become even closer as they have matured. She feels she is not competitive with her twin.

Linda says she doesn't usually enjoy being with her twin, however she feels greater closeness to her twin as she has become older. She does not feel that she has a closer relationship with her twin than with other siblings.

Linda said, "If you were to look at us, you would see nothing that makes us seem alike. But deep down we are maybe too much alike. We have a hard time getting along with each other when we are together for more than a few hours. Perhaps some of this may be jealousy. I have a husband and family and my twin doesn't. But, my twin has her freedom. She can go and do whatever she wants without too much planning or thought. I can't do that."

Jane comments, "I've often thought how my life might have been different. I believe we often did things together at an older age because there existed a feeling that we should like similar things. There were activities that neither one of us tried, probably because our roles were fairly well defined, and though we explored further areas, we stayed pretty close within those roles. This found one or the other not trying out for a sport, or even a class, because the other twin excelled in that area, and we didn't want to play one against the other.

"One instance where I was able to explore what it was like to create an image outside of my 'twin role' and its overriding influence was when I attended a different high school.

"Here I was able to step outside of my role and try my hand at activities I'd been hesitant to try before. I turned out for tennis, the first sport I'd done without my twin following suit. It was *great!* I'm thankful I had that opportunity because it helped me visualize myself as an individual apart from my twin.

"All in all, we've done really well, the two of us exploring life together. I wouldn't trade my twin or our life together away for anything."

Advice to Parents of Twins

To parents of twins Jane says, "Be careful not to generalize. Let each create his own identity. They may appear as being exactly alike, but they will have some differences. Make allowance for this to take place. Being a twin is special! Let their relationship develop between themselves without a lot of fuss.

The advice Jane gives is rich and valuable. "I heartily

recommend that parents of twins get involved in a support group such as the Mothers of Twins clubs. It will always be a lasting experience for me since my mother was an active participant of this wonderful club." She went on to say, "There were many events and lots of childhood friends. The only sad part of this experience is having grown up and being left out on all the news about what those twins and their families are doing. I often thought they should also print an older twins newsletter."

Jane went on to say,"It is so important that twins be seen as separate individuals. Unique as it is to be a twin, it's just as unique to be viewed as a human being, and we all need to know we can make it on our own."

"Don't try to have them do everything alike," writes Linda. "Remember, they are their own person and have their own personalities. I would do as my mother did. Keep them in separate classrooms in school. That way they can express themselves without being afraid their twin will be doing or saying all the same things, or laughing at what their twin had said. It's hard when people laugh at your thoughts. It's crushing when your own family does."

Martha and Kate

These twins were first born, with a younger sister. Martha has twin granddaughters.

Childhood

They were always in the same classroom. They recall being dressed alike as little children but chose not to dress alike when older. They shared a lot of the same playmates.

Martha was not jealous of her twin, did not consider herself the leader, and did not feel in competition. She did not feel less smart, nor was she ever mistaken for her. She did not feel inferior to her twin, nor less attractive. Never did she feel she was being compared by family or friends. This twin did not feel dominated by her twin. They did not share the same bedroom.

Kate was not jealous of her twin, nor did she consider herself the leader. She did not feel competitive with her twin. She did not feel less smart than her twin, however, she felt inferior to her twin. She also felt she was often dominated by her twin. Kate felt she was less attractive than her twin and often felt comparison was made between them.

Martha comments: "I never felt we were compared. We always seemed to be interested in the same things, even sports. We were the first-team tennis doubles (girls) and we played backlot baseball, football, etc. with both boys and girls in our neighborhood. We were even better than some of the boys—not 'little ladies!' We were known as 'the twins.'

"I always felt kind of special for being a twin. When strangers were told we were twins, there was always that 'Oh really!' like they thought that was something special, too. We still get that reaction today.

"My twin and I don't look at all alike, and therefore, unless people are told, there is no way they would ever guess we are twins. They usually say, 'There is a resemblance,' but there really isn't. Of course, I guess they feel they have to say something."

These are the comments Kate shared about being compared: "We look nothing alike. People always tried to find a resemblance, even distant relatives. My mouth was too crowded for my teeth and I had a pinched up mouth, a roman nose. My parents put me in braces for ten years to widen my jaw to let my teeth come in properly, so braces made me very self-conscious. Braces made me a different person as an adult. I am more outgoing now.

"I always had my twin for a 'crutch' at social childhood gatherings. I was glad when she was the leader—then I could stay in the background. I liked that. She was cute and bubbly, and I was not cute and was a rather homely child.

"My mother said I would always let my twin treat me any way she wanted to and I would take it—grab toys, hit me on the head, etc., no matter what. When they'd give us two identical toys or gifts, she would grab mine and trade me and I would let her. My mother said she'd never understood why my twin would do that, or why I would let her."

Parent/Child Relationship

Martha never did feel favoritism was shown by parents. She did not feel comparison was made between her and her twin. She felt her parents dealt with her fairly. She was encouraged to develop her own extracurricular activities.

Martha did add she felt her younger sister "really got away with 'murder' no matter what she did. She usually was able to talk or laugh them out of any punishment. I can remember feeling she was 'spoiled rotten.' Maybe she wasn't, but we felt it; at least I did. Could be that we were two, and she was a single."

Kate did not feel her parents showed favoritism for either of them, nor did they compare them or their performance. She felt she was treated fairly by both parents, and was encouraged to take part in her own extracurricular activities.

She shared this: "My parents tried to force me to be more aggressive. They showed no favoritism that I was aware of. They knew I was introverted and shy and when forced, I stammered. I don't stammer now. They really tried to get me to be more outgoing, but as long as my twin was there, I was content to have her do all the talking."

Adult Relationship

Martha enjoys being with her twin and feels even closer as they have grown older. She feels she knows her twin well and does not feel any competitiveness toward her. She does feel she has compared the performances of her children with that of her twin's children.

Kate enjoys being with her twin and the bond has become even stronger as an adult. She says she feels no competitiveness with her twin. She feels a tighter bond with her twin than with her other sister.

Martha writes, "We have always been close, and best friends, but we always led different lives. Most of our friends were mutual friends, and they still are. That could be because we grew up in this small town, and still live here.

"I read something Kate had written a few years ago. She said I was her best friend. I didn't know that before. She had never told me! It is a nice feeling! I feel the same.

"There have been times when my twin and I will buy the same greeting cards, without previous knowledge. Sometimes we have been known to say the same thing at the same time. Sometimes we will wear outfits that look almost alike."

Kate wrote, "One thing about being a twin is that you don't search for a close friend to tell everything to or to do things with you because you have a 'partner.' At least I did not cultivate my own set of friends. I always had my twin. We were asked to do everything as a pair, whether people wanted to invite both of us or not.

"I was introverted and afraid to be alone with people because I didn't know what to say. I saw to it that she was always there with me. During the war we were separated and I started to 'grow.' I made the hurdle and feel I have a very fulfilling life."

Advice to Parents of Twins

Martha advises, "Love them, and be patient. It really takes patience to get through that first year. Let each twin be his or her own person—not a duplicate of the other twin.

"I just love to dress my twin granddaughters alike, but their mother never does. I guess she is right. It makes sense to me. Just because two kids happen to be born at the same time does not have to mean they must live in the shadow of the other one.

"She is treating them as individuals, with each dressing the way he prefers. When they reach school age she plans to enroll them in different classes, enabling them to express their own individuality. They will have to make their own friends, and express themselves away from each other. I think this is turning out to be the modern way of thinking and raising of twins."

Kate offers this advice to parents of twins. "Subtly, have each go out on his own once in a while to help make them realize they can make it on their own. Start early, like two or three years of age; one going without the other."

Chapter Seven

Opposite Sex Twins

Kirsten and Tim

This set of twins has one older sister and one younger brother.

This set of twins was chosen so that you get a glimpse into the lives of twins where the boy in the set was dominated by the girl. I hasten to add that the gender can be reversed in some opposite sex twin sets. Domination of the girl toward the boy twin is sometimes spoken of as the 'Mother Hen syndrome.' Certainly it is important that parents of twins be alert to what is taking place when they see either twin being dominated.

Childhood

These children were in kindergarten through second grade together, but in separate classes throughout the rest of their school years. One twin felt that their home environment was secure, the other did not feel that way.

Kirsten says she did not feel jealous of her twin. She considered herself the leader. She did not feel competitive with her twin, nor less smart. She did not feel inferior to her twin, nor less attractive. She recalls being dressed alike as small children. Birthdays were always celebrated together.

Kirsten had this to say about comparison. "Because I do not physically resemble my brother, people would ask, 'Are you a twin' or 'Who is your twin?' but I didn't feel positive or negative about the question. I did feel concerned for my brother in that I felt we were compared academically. School was easy for me and he had difficulties."

Tim stated he often felt jealous of his twin, did not consider himself the leader, felt competitive with his twin, and felt less smart. He also felt inferior to his twin, felt less attractive, and felt he was compared with his twin. He felt he was dominated by his twin. About comparison he wrote, "I feel twins, whether opposite sex or same sex twins, are always naturally compared. It is not healthy, but it happens anyway."

These twins had separate bedrooms as they were growing up.

Kirsten reflected on the positives and negatives during childhood years. "I loved walking to school—being in class and walking home with my twin. I remember feeling a bit lonesome when I had to go to a different third grade class. I remember that void—our first separation—for hours. We always shared friends and played together until about twelve years of age. I don't remember anything negative about being a twin, only the positive companionship. Any rivalry that existed was generally between my twin and my younger brother.

"One of my most fond memories is of the first day of kindergarten. Tim and I were all dressed up in fabric which matched his shirt to my very full dress. I remember holding his hand as we walked to school. I also remember feeling very safe and secure with the experience. I do remember another child asking me if I was at all scared. I felt surprised at the question, and stated, 'Of course not, Tim is with me.' It hadn't occurred to me that either of us should be afraid. I'm sure many experiences I went through were less traumatic because I could always count on my companion to be with me. I took this intimate relationship very much for granted until third grade.

"At that time I learned, to my shock, that Tim had been assigned and placed in another classroom. My mother decided to have us in separate classrooms from that time on. It was many years later that she told me our teachers were concerned about our secret language, which only we seemed to understand, and about my dominant behavior in regard to my brother. The school authorities may have been correct in seeing a need for Tim to have some respite from my domination. I can only guess what effect their decision may have had on each of us.

"I do not remember any preparation for this change. I do remember missing Tim terribly during the school day. I remember also worrying about him in third grade, as he had shared with me how mean his teacher, Mrs. Smith, was. She looked mean, and I had heard my mother discussing with the neighbors how school was for Tim. Schooling always seemed more difficult for him. This all seemed like a very mean trick to me. I certainly was not provided any reason for it. In those days, children were mostly just told what the rules were, and that was just the way it was!

"I felt a lot of resentment for the authorities who split us apart. I remember getting in trouble for throwing pinecones at recess that year. I also recall sneaking into the classroom during recess, and stealing my teacher's tools, for example, chalkboard chalk and her grease pencils and red pens. I would hide these items in my underwear, and then throw them away. It was a mystery to the teacher as to who was taking her items, and why her items kept disappearing.

"One day, I recall, she suddenly had us all let her search our desks, coats, and lunch buckets. She was angry, and I remember feeling very afraid I would be identified and humiliated in front of the class. She didn't, however, search our underwear, which is where I temporarily stashed the small items. I noticed she hardly looked at my desk contents. I was never discovered, and am only sharing this story now, after all of these years to illustrate how confused I was. I didn't understand until years later, as an adult, how strong my need must have been to express my anger in some way. I did not cherish, or need, any of the items I stole. I did, however, feel guilty about the thefts for a long time. I have never been tempted to steal anything since that time. I'm sure the guilt wouldn't be worth the cost!

"I hope parents would make any decision to separate twins, in any environment, only after very careful consideration, and that any separations would involve preparation of the children, and a transitional, gradual process would be initiated to avoid any abandonment issues or unnecessary emotional pain to the twins."

Tim shared these thoughts about childhood: "I can remember many times it was difficult for me to 'keep up' with my sister. I remember in second grade I ran home to try and get there before my sister, but she could run faster than I. I got in trouble and my mother called the school and told them we were *never* to be in the same class again. There was never a time in school from that day forward that we were in the same class."

I asked them if there were any experiences they would like to share about their twinship.

Kirsten said, "I remember at the age of thirteen I started menstruating and my brother tackled me and wanted to wrestle. I became very self-conscious and upset to tears before he realized I really meant it. I recall his bewilderment at my not wanting to play and my inability to share with him my need to be 'a girl' and do other things."

Tim commented, "Second grade was a very trying time. We were in the same class and would run home every day and tattle on each other."

Parent/Child Relationship

Kirsten did not feel her parents showed favoritism toward her, nor did she feel her parents showed favoritism toward her twin. She did believe that possibly her parents compared her with her twin brother academically. She thought her parents encouraged her to develop her own extracurricular activities.

Kirsten described her environment as a child. Her mother had a dominant personality. She felt she grew up in a family that cared for each other; however, she noted there was little physical touch or verbal expression of love once she reached the age of four or five.

Tim shared this about his parent/child relationship: "I want to say first that I feel my parents did the best they could to raise us.

"My sister's maturity kept her always one step ahead of me. It was as though she was a whole year ahead of me. I wish my parents had expressed to me the reason I felt like she was always more mature and always one step ahead of me because of the female maturity rate.

"I think my parents had a double challenge in that I had an older sister as well as an 'older' twin sister. I was the oldest boy but that was overshadowed by the above facts.

"I would have benefited from more instruction on dealing with the world—the real world."

Adult Relationship

Kirsten says she enjoys being with her twin brother. She does not feel competitive toward him. She believes she knows her twin well. As an adult she says she feels closer to him than to other siblings.

Kirsten wrote, "I really feel strongly that our companionship at the early stages taught me to love and care for another human being at an early age—maybe sooner than if we had been years apart. We looked out for each other. I could give my brother a bad time, but nobody else better try.

"Looking back as an adult, with my mother as a model, I think I dominated my twin brother too much. Now I feel really bad for men who allow their mate to dominate them in a marriage relationship. I often wonder if my brother would have developed a more assertive, stronger personality if he had not been a twin."

Tim feels he has grown closer to his twin in his adult years. He feels he knows his twin well. He feels he has compared the performance of his children with those of his twin.

Regarding the effect of twinship on him as an adult, he said,

"I would probably be much more assertive. I was very dominated."

Kirsten says, "Tim and I have very different personalities. I suppose, as unique individuals with totally different chromosomes, we're supposed to have these differences. Tim tends to be more passive, much like my father. Due to the conflict and alcohol syndrome dysfunction of the family, I think we are both far too serious, and are only learning now in our mid-life to savor the beauty and laughter of the day as a gift of God.

"My twin brother and I share a lot of the same ideals. I see a lot of differences, but I also see that we have been more alike in our ethics, spiritual faiths, and values than with our other siblings. Perhaps this has been an effect of our early learning and lifelong bonding. We value our children, and our spouses. We've shared our grief. We have long-term marriages. We are honest and loyal. We argue politics and we hug, laugh when we speak, and we can share our victories and some of our vulnerabilities with each other. We can cry, laugh, and pray together. We share. He is my friend, and I hope he knows I am forever his.

"Tim had about an eight-year workaholic lifestyle which included drug and alcohol abuse in his twenties, while I was busy with a new marriage, obtaining a college degree, and the blessings of a new home and motherhood.

"He found sobriety and developed faith in God and shared his changes with me. I realize how alone he must have felt at that juncture in his life. I will always wish we could have nurtured our relationship through those years.

"As adults, we've raised our families, pretty independently. We live in the same state, but with the rush of day-to-day life, we see each other only occasionally. We do communicate by telephone calls and occasional letters. We end our conversations mostly with 'I love you,' and we know that we share a special love. He's a very special person with lots of good qualities. His wife and my two nieces are dear to me.

"Life has brought us a unique bonding experience. For us, the boy and the girl twin. A special gift. We've enjoyed a togetherness, separation, and again a coming together in a matured relationship. Perhaps we can all share in the uniqueness—that special gift that unites us all, and create the desire for understanding ourselves and how we relate to others—*love*."

Advice to Parents of Twins

Kirsten wrote, "Perhaps the best thing my parents did (in the 50's and 60's when I was growing up) in regard to our twinship was to associate with other parents of twins. This led to occasional functions in which we (the entire family) participated, integrating with other sets of twins. This taught me that, although twinship was unique, we were not odd, or alone in the experience. I am sure the meetings my mother attended faithfully for over thirty years were of assistance to her as well.

"Another point I'd like to share, would be the hope that parents of opposite sex twins take time to learn how to prepare their twins for the changes which occur naturally with the arrival of puberty. I remember no such preparation. I doubt that many parents at that time thought about it. If I felt abandonment in second grade, alone in a room full of children, then I'm sure Tim must have felt something comparable when I suddenly never wanted to wrestle with him, or play in the woods, and other daily activities we used to share. At twelve, I began giving my attention to girl friends, and later, to boyfriends. Suddenly, almost overnight, I had no interest in him or his interests. He seemed years behind in maturity. I remember at this time he began competing with our younger brother in many ways. They became the 'boys' and my sister and I were the 'girls,' although my sister insisted that we three younger children were all 'the kids.'

"I do remember my father suddenly blurting out to me one day that I should consider Tim's feelings, and telling me that because of my behavior, Tim was having a hard time. I remember feeling resentful that my father was trying to make me feel guilty for dating. I don't remember any further discussion. But then, there wasn't a lot of discussion in the family. We could have benefited from some guidance and counseling to help us share our feelings on the matter. In our family, children were to be seen but not heard, not a healthy attitude, but perhaps more prevalent in the 50's and 60's.

"I would encourage parents to engage in open communication with each of their children. This needs to be initiated in the early developmental years, so each child feels a sense of trust, and knows his feelings will be validated.

"This will prepare them to better exercise their feelings with a trusted adult and help them sort out what they are feeling, should they experience abandonment issues, or have any confusion about their twin relationship.

"Parents should familiarize themselves with signals of stress in their children. They should be ready to assist and guide them with information and counseling, if necessary, to ease each child with developmental changes. These changes become very noticeable in the twin experience. It is a very confusing time for all children, this prepuberty/puberty stage! Boy/girl twin relationships need nurturing during the preteen and teen years— and each should be encouraged. Their relationship will have its ups and downs like any intimate relationship, but it will survive and grow if it is nurtured.

"Every child needs a sense of autonomy. Parents of multiples should avoid comparing their twins to each other, and to their siblings. Siblings do enough 'measuring up' themselves. My mother was always comparing and labeling each of us. 'That's my healthy one,' 'That's the student, there,' and 'This is my artistic one,' 'This is my obstinate one.' Such remarks lend themselves to wedges psychologically driven between parent and child and between siblings.

"I remember adults asking me quite seriously if my brother and I were identical. Occasionally, people still ask me! As a child, I can remember feeling slightly embarrassed for them, as I explained that Tim was a boy and I was a girl. In those days, boys and girls dressed very differently. Besides that fact, Tim and I have different builds, (more evident now than as children), and vastly different colorings of our skin, hair and eyes!

"One of my most treasured pictures is a small black and white which was taken on our tenth birthday. We were best buddies then. We learned to ride bikes, climb trees, skip rope, throw hoops and hula hoop, fish, build forts, light matches and make newspaper torches. We learned to dig for razor clams and learned to swim like fish. A long time has passed since then. We grew apart in many ways."

Kirsten wrote, "I would tell parents to discuss twinship with all of their children. Explain that people are each unique. Also, if two active children cause stress on either parent, the parent must take time to find a way to relieve the stress, rather than take it out on the children."

Tim wrote, "Don't compare. We are each different with different ideas."

Bob and Anne

No other siblings.

Reading about this set of twins will give you a feel for the importance of seeing your twin children as individuals who have been born with their own uniqueness. The boy in this set was born with a penchant for drawing and has lived his life as a card designer for a large greeting card company. As you read, you will see that it was competition that made being a twin difficult. Neither of these people has given much thought to his twinship and the effect it may have had upon his life.

These twins grew up in a two-parent family and both felt their home was emotionally secure. These twins viewed themselves as being quite different from one another. Both felt their personalities were nothing alike. In reviewing the questionnaires of these twins it appears that, not only did the boy feel less attractive than his twin, she also felt less attractive.

Childhood

Bob was second-born. He remembers being dressed alike when small, and recalls usually being given similar toys and gifts as a small child. He was often jealous of his twin and felt in competition with her. He did not feel dominated by his twin. They did not share the same bedroom as children.

Bob had this to say about childhood and comparison:

"I was constantly compared, especially in school. I attribute my early stuttering problem to this comparison. We had every class together through high school. My sister was what every teacher dreamed of having in their class. My interest was in cartooning since I was two years old and I was not a good student until my college years when I was allowed to grow as an individual."

When asked to respond to positives or negatives in childhood regarding twinship Bob wrote, "My twin and I had nothing in common."

Anne does not recall being dressed alike as small children, nor did she ever want to dress alike. She often felt jealous of her twin and felt in competition with him. She also felt inferior to her twin as well as thinking of herself as less attractive. She also felt somewhat dominated by her twin brother.

Anne made this comment about her feelings of being compared: "As a child I was hurt because my mother always told everybody how artistic my brother was and showed his drawings. I had nothing to show. I was always just 'a good kid.'"

She shared this about the positives or negatives of being a twin in childhood. "Having the same group of friends was a negative because my brother always teased me and they would laugh. It made me feel very inferior and as a result I always worried about what people thought of me. I still do!"

Parent/Child Relationship

Bob felt his mother showed favoritism toward his sister as well as compared his performance against hers.

Anne also felt favoritism was shown her twin by their mother and that comparison was evident to some degree. She did not feel that punishment was administered fairly by the mother.

She made this comment as she reflected back upon childhood and her relationship with her parents. "I felt my mother really catered to my brother and that he could do no wrong. I hated him at the time for getting away with it and her for not caring as much about me. It hurt because I always did so much to please."

Adult Relationship

Both of these people, as adults, said they usually enjoy being with their twin. As adults both said they no longer feel competitive toward one another.

Do they feel being a twin has had a definite upon their personality? Bob wrote, "Yes. The fact that I stuttered forced me to express myself visually rather than verbally." Anne said, "Perhaps. Trying so hard to be liked—I'm still that way."

Advice to Parents of Twins

Bob offers these suggestions:

1. Don't take advantage of their 'twinness' for your own ego.

2. Encourage individuality but don't discourage sameness if they choose to dress alike, etc.

3. Don't make comparisons, or allow others to do it.

To school officials he made this comment, "Allow more flexibility in the schools toward twins. If parents feel separation would be advantageous to individual growth, school boards should allow this."

Anne offered this to parents of twins, "Let them be themselves, more so if they are identical."

Janet and Mark

These twins had two older brothers in family.

Here you will read about twins who are working to establish a warmer relationship with one another. In responding to the questionnaire, one remarked that he was surprised that he was able to recall incidents that took place between him and his twin sister when they were small. They seemed appreciative of the opportunity to reflect upon their childhood as twins.

Since the girl in this set was the only girl in the family, her twin felt that much favoritism was shown. It would appear that favoritism was a detrimental factor in their relationship.

Childhood

These twins report that their childhood was not very stable emotionally; however, they did grow up in a two-parent family until the death of their mother when they were fifteen.

They were in the same classroom through the fifth grade.

Janet wrote, "My brother and I were born into a home with two older brothers who were in their teens. I was the favorite as the only girl in the family. As we grew up, I became the 'fixer,' the obedient child, never making waves, getting good grades, taking care of everybody! My brother, well, he became the 'clown,' the attention-getter, rebellious and frustrated. Everyone would say that I had it so together. 'Whatever happened to your brother?' I'm sure this had a lot of bearing on my twin's outlook and how we learned to deal with things. I grew up feeling I could take care of myself, as though I didn't need anyone. My twin grew up blaming everyone for what happened to him."

Janet continued, "I grew up giving; he grew up taking. We have stayed close in spite of this, but suffered many years not understanding each other, trying to convince ourselves we were right, the other one mixed up!

"I went through alcohol treatment several years ago and this has helped me have a pretty clear understanding of myself and all my relationship issues. I am now able to let my twin be who he is. I don't have to fix him anymore!"

Janet considered herself very much the leader during childhood. She felt she was not as smart as her twin.She did not feel she was in competition with her twin, nor did she feel inferior to him. As children they shared the same room.

As Mark reflected upon his childhood he said he often felt jealous of his twin. He did not consider himself the leader. He did feel he was in competition with his twin.

Janet said this about comparison. "At times I felt comparison during young adolescence due in part to an aunt who was highly educated and pointed out our weaknesses and strengths."

Mark was most adamant when he said, "Yes, I felt compared. Teachers would say, 'Why can't you do as well as your sister?' I very much resented being compared. I am actually more intelligent but had no drive as our Dad's booze and browbeating took away my self-esteem in about the third grade. From then on I stopped trying, as I believed I was a loser."

Recalled Incidents as Children

Mark recalled this happening during his childhood. He wrote, "Once at age four or five, my twin fractured her elbow. As a result the other kids on our street set up a lemonade stand and gave my sister the proceeds, $1.62. (I can't believe I remember this.) I thought somehow I should have shared in her windfall but she made a big deal out of how she did not have to share any of it, and didn't."

Janet wrote, "I feel very badly at times that my brother felt so terribly inferior to me. As he has grown older, he appears to be self-driven to 'out do' whatever he feels I have achieved, i.e., going to college, making more money, etc. It seem to be too much a part of his motivation to prove himself. To prove not only to himself, but to prove it to me."

Parent/Child Relationship

These children were a surprise to these parents who were in their early forties. Their mother suffered a stroke when they were small and died when they were teenagers.

Mark wrote that their father took to the bottle, brought on, he felt, in great part because of their mother's condition.

Alcohol made the father abusive, which resulted in Mark saying that "Dad called me about everything one could. As a result he tore me down to the point that I believed what he said. I learned years later that I did not have to spend my life proving he was right. In my late twenties I began building my self esteem."

Mark felt his sister was the favorite since she was the only girl in the family. He felt because of this she was able to 'get away' with a lot more than he.

Janet said, "He used me as a mother substitute for many years, therefore I gave him advice as asked for, and he became dependent on me. One day recently he woke up and started (at forty) to make decisions! It's great! He hates me now, but I don't care, because I never did want, nor did I ask for that role! I just saw it happening! Therefore my answers will reflect we could, at this time, have had enough of each other."

Adult Relationship

Do these twins enjoy being together now, as adults? Mark said, "As long as Janet doesn't offer unsolicited advice." The other felt their relationship could be much improved.

Both of these people say they have not compared the performances of their children with their twin's children. Mark felt he did not know his twin well. Janet felt that she knows her twin well.

As Mark assessed his feelings he said he now feels "I am my own man."

Regarding communication, Janet said, "There is a trust and kinship that comes from our early bonding that seems to ever be present in our relationship. It is a feeling that cannot be felt with other siblings—it is special and unique to my twin and me. I believe that this early bonding has been the mainstay of our relationship and ability to communicate openly. Even when we are at opposites and do not agree philosophically or otherwise, we seem to have a clear understanding of where the other is coming from. It may be in part because of our closeness. We are more honest with one another. I feel more free to be myself because I've already been in vulnerable positions and don't have to protect myself as much."

Advice to Parents of Twins

Here is what these twins have to say to parents:

Mark wrote "As it says in Proverbs 22:6, 'Train up a child in the way he should go.' In other words, treat them as though they had separate identities, for they do." Janet wrote "Ignore or avoid the twin routine as much as possible. Make them feel as totally individual as possible. Allow them to develop their own personalities. Dress individually as they become aware, and separate in classrooms from the beginning."

Janet wrote, "The healthiest thing that could possibly be done to help twins bond (or any child for that matter) is to raise them in an atmosphere of love, honesty, trust, and to enrich their sense of self-esteem and self-worth. Never, never compare one to the other as 'better than,' but build and support each child's special talents and needs.

"I think twins have an uncanny ability to bond themselves, without anyone's help. The mere fact they are the same age, going through the same growth patterns, forces the bonding without anyone's help or particular encouragement. Personally I am not sure that 'pushing' the issue would be particularly healthy.

"The healthiest thing that could possibly be done to help bond twins or siblings is to raise them in an atmosphere of love, honesty, trust and to enrich their sense of self esteem and self worth. Never, never compare one to the other as 'better than,' but to build and support each child's special talents and needs.

"Ignore or avoid the twin routine as much as possible and

make them feel as totally individual as possible. Allow them to develop their own personalities. Dress them individually as they become aware, and separate in classrooms from the beginning."

The material you've just read from these twins expresses their feelings when they were in their early forties. Now they are sharing their thoughts twelve years later.

Mark shared this, "At the time when I first wrote to you I loved my twin but had gotten to the point where I was avoiding contact with her as she seemed to criticize everything my wife and I did. Then one day she called and asked if we'd been trying to call her. She told me she had been in an alcohol treatment center. Almost overnight she changed. She no longer offered unsolicited advice and went out of her way to be kind. She and her husband have developed many new friendships. My sister now plays hostess to the best of holiday gatherings I've ever seen. She befriends practically anyone. She's become a very gregarious person.

"Three years ago I fell off a ladder, breaking my wrist and severing an artery. By morning I was $12,000 in debt and no insurance. It looked as though Christmas would be very bleak indeed. However, that was not the case. My twin asked for my children's Christmas list and took care of it. What would have been an awful holiday turned out to be one of the best. Then on my next birthday she offered to take my family to Disneyland the next summer! This was something we could never afford."

He adds, "Our relationship has much improved over the last few years."

Nora and John

These twins were sandwiched in between three older brothers, two older sisters and two younger sisters.

These twins was chosen from many sets of opposite sex twins because their responses to the questionnaire had all the responses that foster a healthy relationship between twins.

Childhood

They grew up in a two-parent family and both felt their childhood was emotionally secure. They attended the same school and were in the same classroom until the beginning of third grade. They shared many of the same playmates and both recall being dressed alike as small children.

Since both of these people marked their 'Yes/No' answers the same, I will tell you that neither of them felt jealousy toward one another. They did not feel in competition with the other, nor felt that one was smarter than the other. Neither twin felt inferior nor dominated, however the girl did say that she often considered herself the leader. The boy did feel that he was less attractive than his sister during childhood. They did not share a bedroom.

John had this to say about comparison: "I never remember any when my twin sister and I were compared. My twin and I grew up being very close to each other and we are still this way. I feel very privileged to have a twin sister."

Nora said this about comparison. "My parents raised us as individuals and usually I felt towards my brother like I did the other three, that I had four brothers. I never felt compared by family members or friends. Sometimes I would get tired of being referred to as 'the twins.'"

Parent/Child Relationship

The responses from these twins are identical as they looked back over their relationship with their parents. They felt any punishment was administered fairly. Each was encouraged to develop his own interests in and out of school. There was a twinge of favoritism felt by the girl which was evident due to a bicycle accident in which her brother was critically injured.

Nora wrote, "After my brother's accident I felt my mother was overprotective of him for quite some time. I felt they worried more about him than they did me. I remember realizing how fortunate we all were that he lived, so I seemed to understand. I think my sister two years older felt left out a lot due to attention we received from relatives and friends. My mother enjoyed children so much that we did receive wonderful care."

John wrote this as he reflected upon his childhood and his relationship with his parents.

"I remember one morning when my twin and I were probably five or six years old, we decided we wanted chicken for dinner. We asked Mom, and she said she did not have time to fix them. So Nora and I went out to the chicken coop and killed four chickens. We did get chicken for dinner that day."

"I feel I have the best parents in the world. They have done so much for my brothers and sister and myself. I know we will never be able to pay them back.

"I think having twins is one of the nicest things that can happen to parents expecting children. I, being a parent, would have been proud to have had twins in our family," wrote John.

Adult Relationship

These twins live far apart, and are happy when they do get together. There is no competitiveness between them. Both feel they know one another well.

Nora writes that she enjoys telling people she is a twin. She says, "I don't think about it often, but when I do I realize it's special. We always call each other on our birthday."

Twelve years later I made contact with John and Nora and they gave me an update on their lives and their relationship with one another. John wrote mostly about the accident that happened to him when he was only seven. He now realizes the impact his accident had upon the other members of his family. He wrote, "I feel at times that my siblings were jealous of all the presents I got and the money I got from friends, aunts, and uncles." Yet, he went on to speak of the love he feels within his family. He is confident that there is no resentment within his family for the extra show of affection that he received.

As his twin sister reflected on the shower of attention given her twin brother she does recall that as a child she thought he was spoiled. Now many years later, she understands the extra attention was a vital part of her twin brother's recovery and she is grateful for any act that helped her brother gain back his health.

She says she will always feel special being a twin, but she continued she said, "As I grow older and we are apart, I really don't think very often about being a twin."

Advice to Parents of Twins

John wrote, "Love them both the same and treat them as individuals."

Nora said, "I would think it best to raise them as brothers and sisters and not refer to them as 'the twins.'

"It's important to discover their individual personalities. Parents can do a lot. I think dressing twins alike and always wanting them to be together is odd. I think it's harder to think of them as individuals."

Sarah and Nathan

This set of twins grew up surrounded by three brothers and three sisters, all older.

The mother of this set of twins left her family for another man when they were six months old. The father, a minister with a great amount of tenacity, was determined to keep his family together even though members of his congregation offered to adopt some of the children. There were suggestions that some of them be placed in a Christian Childrens Home. The father was adamant about keeping them all together.

Childhood

Both of these twin children responded the same to all of the childhood questions asked in the questionnaire, except for one. Nathan said he often considered himself the leader. There were no signs of jealousy, competition, feelings of inferiority, nor expressions of competition between them. Neither said he was dominated by the other.

Nathan said this about comparison, "We were proud to be noticed and discussed as twins: our likenesses and differences."

Sarah wrote regarding her feelings about their being compared, "I never felt we were being compared. We were both treated equally and neither of us got anything without the other getting the same, or something equal to the other's gift."

As these twins reflected back upon their childhood they had this to say, Nathan wrote, "My protective responsibility for my sister seemed very strong, but accepted with fearless pride."

Sarah wrote, "I felt closer to my twin than to my other sisters and brothers, however, I love all my siblings very much. I always felt that if anything ever happened to my twin brother I wouldn't want to live. Now that we're married and have children I still love him and he's very special to me. I have a wonderful husband and four daughters and grandchildren, but I still feel especially close to my twin and we still love to get together, play our instruments, sing and do things with our families."

Parent/Child Relationship

Both of them said they felt there was no favoritism shown them. They said they did most everything together, yet did not feel they were compared as to their performance. These twins enjoyed being together. Sarah said neither of them wanted to go someplace without the other also being able to go. Sarah continued, "We worked on a 480-acre truck farm my father owned. We all worked together raising fruits, vegetables and running a wood yard. When we got tired, our father would blow a police whistle and call all of us in to rest, then we'd all go back to work. He worked with us in the kitchen and helped us younger girls with the meals and the dishes when the older girls married and left home. He was a very special person in our lives and we all loved him for the real man—and father and mother—that he was. He always had time to play with us, take us on picnics, fishing, swimming, play dominoes or anything else we wanted to do. Papa said God gave him his children and he would work day and night to keep us together."

Nathan wrote, "Our father worked hard to keep us in school, working all hours, was very loving and encouraged us to sing duets in harmony and was proud of us. With him having only a fifth grade education, finances for all our needs were very low. Our mother left us and our father for another man when we were six months old and this had a negative effect on all the children in general. The oldest was sixteen years old. But our father kept us together and did his best. No mother could have more love for their children. This gave me a greater love for my family and other people as a whole."

Adult Relationship With Twin

As these twins reflected back upon their adult feelings toward their twin, only pride and love come through. There is no sign of competitiveness. They have always felt very much connected to one another and it has continued into their adult lives.

Nathan wrote, "I feel closer to her than to other siblings. It was a pleasure having someone my age and with many feelings in common."

Sarah said, "I don't think we could be any closer. I don't think I could have handled the difficulties and challenges in life had it not been for the strength my twin gave me and I gave him. Our twinship kept us together through our tears, sadness, loss of mother, sisters and brothers as they married and left home. We had each other to lean on, something we neither one had with our siblings."

Advice to Parents of Twins

Nathan offers this advice, "Keep them close as much as possible. Dress them alike if possible and make them proud of their heritage."

Sarah wrote, "Encourage them to be their own selves and do things on their own. Don't make them dress alike if they do not choose to do so. Don't show partiality; remember, when you offend one twin you hurt the other twin. They will stick together no matter what happens."

Childhood and Twinhood

The following is a chapter from Lillian Baker's book, Reflections, Past and Present, *about her childhood as an opposite sex twin. It is included here with the author's permission. Lillian Baker is author-historian-lecturer.*

It is only by reflecting back in maturity that one can evaluate certain incidents and happenings, causes and effects, without the issue becoming clouded by prejudice and childish emotions. And because of my maturity I have such a different outlook and understanding of my childhood and my twin-hood...for I was a twin, and being a twin affected my childhood considerably. Maybe the effect would not have been as considerable if we had been identical twins in any respect, that is if we were of the same sex or degree of intelligence or similar in personality or nature. No twins born could have been so opposite and yet so devoted. I won't use the term 'love' because I don't want to be one-sided about that issue. My brother was and always will be a cynic and even today I think he would be offended by the use of the sentimental term of 'love.' So I will settle for the term 'affectionate' because in very devious ways and always trying to cover up any obvious display of such emotion, my twin gave me just enough affection at the right psychological moment for me to want nothing more than to live in his esteem and for him to be my sovereign. I, so unlike him, could not be an entity within myself. Where I lacked aggressiveness, he had enough to dominate his schoolmates and his teachers and even his family. Where I lacked self-confidence, his ego was abetted by his superior grades in school and his scientific mind that was always on the search for cool-headed logic which made my own answers based on natural emotion seem too simple to be correct. I was only too eager to give him the floor as were others, for there was no doubt that he absorbed book knowledge like a sponge, languages came to him as easy as ABC, and in addition, he had the amiable good looks of a rascal, the tall stature to give any man extra confidence (though Lord knows he had enough of that!) and enough vanity to stay aloof, which only made him more desirable to both sexes and all ages. Yes, this was my twin, and I was his shadow.

It may sound preposterous, but we never quarrelled in childhood! Now I realize it was because I was too meek, afraid if I did not agree, my replies would sound ignorant...afraid he would use words that I did not understand then, and therefore had to be accepted as the truth, for I (like so many others) was too prone to accept that which I did not understand as the truth. Besides, I felt so completely rejected and outside my own family circle, I could not bear the thought of jeopardizing my position of jester in the 'king's court,' for I can remember happily now that the one thing I *was* able to do was to bring enough wit to dull the sharpness of sarcasm. That was my usual way of apologizing for him to family or friends when his acid tongue hit its mark. I never felt the effects of his biting remarks personally, but because I react emotionally to the feelings of others, I suffered with them but could not join them in what I knew would be a useless argument. He inevitably was the winner and in most cases he was strong enough in victory to bring the captives along with him for another ride to the next dispute. People could not help but admire his capacity for learning and his oratory ability. Shortly after we entered elementary school, he left me behind scholastically and finally graduated a full year ahead of me as valedictorian of his class.

Although he was in none of my classes, we walked to school

together, ate our lunches together, and met after school for a daily trade of treats at the ice cream parlor. One day I bought and the next day he did. He always had buddies trailing along, but I held prime place by his right side and proudly followed the master and his pupils, for the truth was that he was always a good teacher even before he became one professionally. It wasn't until he graduated from high school and went into college that I was finally on my own, and then out of emotional necessity I made my first real friends who have remained thus throughout my life. These friends became my second family. My girl friend was in one of my classes. She asked me home one day and I met her family. I became one of them. Here was a family so unlike my own...simple, not complex...peaceful and content, instead of the constant clashing of minds and personalities...surrounded by books and music, instead of plush unusable parlors...the sharing of love and mutual admiration, instead of fierce competition. So I left my native soil which was actually foreign to me and found myself in sweet harmony with a new family who accepted an ouside runt into the litter just as they would have accepted as many as need be. They had enough warmth and affection to share, and this they did willingly. I owe them much for helping me through the period when my twin was gone and I felt so deserted and alone and too weak to cope with what I never had to understand...faced with making decisions I never had to make before. My girl friend who took me home with her that day confessed many years later that the invitation was extended on a whim because she said she always felt so sorry for me. It seemed I was always so alone and shy. I looked so lost. Well, I was. I was alone as far as people were concerned, but I had the company of good books from the library, and good music on the radio, and a tremendous imagination. My imagination no doubt had much to do with my magnifying small hurts and shuns as magnitudes of oppression. I often wondered as I thought about my brother and others who drew people to them like flies to honey...what is it like to be liked? I never took the next step of asking myself why I didn't find out for myself. I had already convinced myself I was defeated and cheated. I was the afterbirth, the afterthought of my twin, and I had to make the best of it, that's all! So I became probably the youngest recluse, living in my cave of books and enjoying my stolen moments with the family radio listening to concerts. (This kind of music was like a funeral dirge to them.) To me music has and always will be my first love. With my adopted family, I came into the wide world of music through their record collection and one of the first things I purchased when I went out on my own was a small radio and a wind-up phonograph. Then came my record collection which is now enviable and still one of my greatest sources of pleasure.

It was with the departure of my twin to college that I also sought refuge in writing my thoughts on paper. My other brothers and sisters had become strangers to me. We had no common meeting ground of thoughts. Before this time, I would write imaginary stories, fairy tales, and dreamy poetry, but I soon found a release in putting down my reactions to incidents that really happened. With nobody to tell them to, I would get emotional release by putting the story on paper. The only brother besides my twin who might have become close to me and who was really most like me personality-wise, had left home himself when he was sixteen. He, too, had graduated well ahead of his classmates and was already out into the world finding his place. He was called the 'black sheep' of the family. I was the lily-white-lamb who followed obediently. As a matter of fact, I was the only one who meekly obeyed every command of my parents, and submitted to the whims of the others for fear of an angry outburst. I have always had a horror of loud angry voices and scenes, and would become physically ill in my room when they occurred. Even though an incident did not involve me, I could not help being involved emotionally and it has never been in my make-up to accept violence without a mental and physical reaction. I abhor it! I can recall when rather that have my mother's temper taken out on my younger sister (who could match tempers on an even scale with her), I would put myself between them and suffer the wrath of both. When my mother would vent her temper with a whipping, I would stifle my cries because somehow inside I felt that she hated what she was doing and that she would really suffer with me if I let her know how much it really hurt. And I did not want her to suffer. Now, as I look back, this was more true than I was willing to accept later when a breach occurred between us that took almost a decade to mend...and then never fully. When a heart is broken, it can be mended but there is always a crack that even scar tissue cannot cover.

For many years I could not understand what had really happened to create an abnormal feeling between mother and daughter. I can never once remember showing her disrespect while I was at home with her, and she always admitted to this. Now I can understand that we simply never had the understanding or the meeting of the minds. She, like my twin, could not think or comprehend on my level. There was no meeting of the minds then, and there is and never will be now.But I have understanding, and understanding and maturity can do much to open one's eyes to basic facts.

To say I never loved my mother would be a gross understatement. Up to the age of twelve, I worshipped her! Then, because of an incident, this idolization was completely transferred to my twin. How unfortunate for both her and me! I heard an expression once: 'Is it my words, or your ears?' ... by this I mean to point out that I don't really know if it was simply that we were at the opposite ends of the poles emotionally or if it was complete misunderstanding on both our parts. It seemed that she was incapable of understanding or accepting my affection, and I in turn was too easily offended and hurt by the slightest shun on her part. She was a woman of many moods, easy tantrums, and of great vanity. She was also a woman who was glorified by my father and feared by him too. He and I were so much alike...poor soul...he could never have a common meeting ground with her either. Yet through it all he adored her and respected her as the mother of his children, and not once did he ever vilify her (right or wrong), and this he did at the sacrifice of his own great need for love. Oh such a pity and waste! What a basically warm person he was, and how smothered he became by her nature and domination. Oh why could she not have known that everything a person really needed was within the walls of her own home?

Looking back on many incidents, I realize I learned from my own childhood experiences how to cope with my own motherhood. I can't help comparing: I could have been no more than seven or eight when I gave up my penny candy to a young boy who had what I considered a most precious bullfrog. I wanted to surprise my mother with a gift. It was no special occasion. I was a perpetually affectionate child to anyone who wished to be a recipient. I wonder now why I wasn't discouraged by her before this...but then she was my mother and I adored her. She was the most beautiful woman in the world to me. She sang like an angel when she floated from one room to another. And she was different than ordinary mothers, I thought. Other mothers always had on unattractive house dresses and aprons, and looked very drab. My mother dressed in chiffon and wore jewelry, and had exquisite auburn hair with natural waves glistening gold when the sunlight fell upon it, and she had violet eyes fringed with dark lashes and accentuated by dark well-shaped brows! She lived in a secret room off to one side of the house and never emerged except in a luxurious dressing gown smelling heavenly, and always with her porcelain skin aglow with nature's own blush of good health. She was always like a flower in full bloom! Always so perfect in my childish innocent eyes so willing to accept beauty on the surface without looking any deeper. Now I realize it was because of this innocence that I could not accept her ugly temper as being part of this beautiful being whom I called 'mother.' Anyway, I put the bullfrog where she was sure to find it, and when I insisted that it was a gift and not a prank I was not believed. She rejected it and me in no uncertain terms. I begged forgiveness in a poem titled "To My Angel Mother" and painted it with hearts and flowers. I really wooed her for affection that should not have needed wooing. I thought of the frog incident when my son brought one home to me from a neighborhood pond. My first impulse was of revulsion, but this was curbed by the natural joy of receiving any gesture from my children of affection, whether it be by word, demonstration, or gift. So this frog my son brought me as a gift lived in my small garden and I consoled myself with the fact that it actually ate insects, or so I convinced myself, and my fear of insects is greater than my fear of frogs.

One thing I remember very vividly about my mother was her abhorrence of being touched...of having physical contact with me. I can never remember ever being held in her arms. When she did approach me, it was on her volition and it was always she who made the overture. She wanted or showed no need of response. The very last time I ever had any physical contact with my mother in terms of affection was when I was twelve years old. I remember the incident so distinctly that every time I think of it I re-live the hurt and bewilderment and rejection. If ever there was a trauma in my childhood that affected my whole future, this was it! I was seated on a small couch in a sitting room in our home. I was waiting for her to come out of her dressing room. She was going to an affair with my father. (He was always so proud of her, almost as though she were a prized jewel!) I sat by myself. The other children never seemed to be as taken with either her beauty or presence as I was. I waited for the 'vision' to appear. And appear it did! She was wearing a lavender, white, and black silk-chiffon print dress and a wide-brimmed straw hat. The hat was white, had a black band, and a bunch of violets on the side. The violets matched her eyes. I remember thinking that I had never seen anything so beautiful and I felt so full of adoration and love. I knew that I should not touch but I could not control myself. I leaped from the couch and in an instant had my arms around her neck. She was furious! I had messed her hair and set her hat askew! Didn't I know enough not to touch her when she was all dressed? I retired to my room like a whipped puppy, tail between its legs and consoling itself with quiet whimpers. As usual, my father came in and made some lame apology for her actions. But I never touched her again, and with that rejection it seemed a door closed on a section of my heart which had until then been reserved solely for her.

Now, after so many years, I still cannot have any physical contact with her because although perhaps now she would enjoy the display of affection, I cannot do so without restraint. I fight it off, or try to, with a mature mind but it is there nevertheless. I am ashamed of this feeling. I have no desire to hurt her. I never have wanted to. I find it so easy now to make allowances I could not make for such a long time. With maturity and understanding I realize that she could no more help being herself than I can help being myself. As a matter of fact, I have done more damage to myself trying to undo myself than in trying to be myself. They say my mother has not changed, yet I can now accept her as a person, an individual, and with due respect because she carries the title 'mother' and she was instrumental in giving me the life I consider precious. I have learned with maturity that mother-love is not something that automatically arrives with childbirth. I learned that all women are not maternal. My own childhood experience have served me well and prepared me all the better for the responsibilities of my own motherhood and in my attitude toward my children.

I wish it had been possible to write of my childhood memories as a series of bedtime stories, excitement, adventure, and so forth…like the childhood dreams I read so much about and hear so much about from my own children. But I cannot. Most of my childhood has been willfully blanked out or rejected. Many childhood reactions and naivete were experienced after I was already out of high school and on my own. How naive and immature I was! What childish bitterness and determination! How unprepared I was for the deep water when I had hardly been able to wade in by myself unaccompanied by my twin! And with so little foundation of faith and love to act as a buoy at high tide!

Still it seems that from the moment I took the leap there was always a strong swimmer by my side and enough faith and common sense to accept help when I was caught in strong undertow. So I eventually became quite an excellent swimmer in the sea of life (come high or ebb tide), and although many of my strokes have been uneven and ungraceful, I am able to buck the tide, and when I have felt overwhelmed or exhausted I have enough sense to turn and rest, floating on my back as it were. And I relax knowing I am not alone. I think it was during these periods of rest, floating on my back with my eyes closed to everything, that I matured and reached a certain philosophy and deep faith. Sometimes closed eyes see more clearly.

My twin and I have both matured each in our own way. We lead completely different lives with a different sense of values and still share no common philosophy or faith. At long last I have a separate identity, and I think now he really loves me and respects me more for it. (Maybe in truth I was the burden to him.) Yes, I think somehow he has finally learned to love me, too. And mature love is, after all, the most fulfilling.

Reflections No. 1

Chapter Eight

Relationship with Siblings

The long-awaited birth of their second child was about to happen. The mother had included their two-and-a-half year old daughter in all the preparations that had taken place for the welcoming of their new baby. Excitement ran high for all the family, including grandparents, aunts and uncles. Delivery day arrived, but instead of the one they had all expected, two showed up. The shock, yes, almost unbelief, put everyone in a new mode of thinking.

The emotions from the various members of the family ran from jubilation to fear. The little girl who had so anxiously waited the arrival of a little brother or sister learned she had two to help care for and entertain. She had been told by her mother she would be her little helper and that had pleased her. She was doubly happy for a while, but jubilation over the birth of two did not last as she gradually began to realize she was no longer the center of attention. The babies were. She observed that Mommy and Daddy no longer had time to give her. Time that had always been hers. They were too busy taking care of the new babies.

It is always fortunate if a family can know early on when twins are expected so they can prepare not only themselves, but their children as well.

It has been my observation that the number of children in a

family and the ages of the children when twin children arrive, play a significant role in how the singletons are affected by the arrival of twins.

I have noticed it is usually an only child around two or three years of age, who appears at greatest risk for having a more difficult time accepting the arrival of twins. Up to this time this little child has been the center of attention. Now he observes two little bodies who seem to capture all the comments, smiles and attention.

It is not unusual for these little ones, who are just beginning to define themselves, to suddenly become totally different after the birth of twins. They may show their resentment by being rebellious. They may even show anger toward the new babies who have taken over their territory.

It is important for parents to give special attention to the older child during this period. By giving extra attention during these early days, parents will usually be rewarded with much better behavior. Little ones who have been upstaged by twins are too young to understand the extra demands that have been placed upon their parents. It is only the parents' actions toward them that will assure them they are equally loved.

Here is a letter from a woman who shared her thoughts about the arrival of twins into her family. As you can tell, their appearance appears to have had a lifelong effect upon her life.

"In reply to your questionnaire on twins, let me tell you that the sibling rivalry continued almost from the cradle until the present day. I was only ten-and-one-half-months old when the twins were born, so their presence made no difference to me until I was old enough to understand their overpowering and intimidating attitude towards me.

"They knew they were the center of attraction, favored by my mother who doted on them. My father, on the other hand, who loved me with an overwhelming obsession, restored a profound balance in my life. However, they caused me to become an introvert, a lonely child who had no other sister or brother to console me when I was verbally and physically abused by the twins who were worlds apart in our characters. I was sensitive and profoundly spiritual, yet, I was perceptive in more ways than they. In fact, they acted as a catalyst in my search for an inner strength. Family and friends doted on them—I hardly existed in the eyes of those who would exclaim, "Oh, the twins are beautiful," etc. I was the ugly duckling, unattractive with no great physical attributes. I played make-believe games with myself when I was the only actor on center stage. I loved playing the heroine, a role which gave me great satisfaction due to the lack of love I had experienced as a child.

"My sisters had strong characters, very strong, and I always felt humbled in their presence. I ran away from home at the age of ten and lived with my grandparents, aunt and uncle, an extended family, helping to raise my aunt's eight brats. But I loved my independence and cherished it above all else, for I was part of a happy family life.

"My sisters and I were strangers, always ignoring each other when we were reunited. My sense of values were different than theirs. Whereas I was a plain Jane, they were models of fashion. My tastes were simple, theirs extravagant because our mother lavished them with the best things in life, which I did not deny them. They were socialites, while I stood in my little corner, the spotlight always on them. They are artists while I'm in the literary field. They enjoy a lavish lifestyle, both married to professionals. I married a peasant by choice. We differed in our tastes of husbands. I reared my kids in virtual poverty; theirs were raised in an affluent society.

"I have no malice in my heart and soul towards them. They made it in life. And so did I in my own way. I gratefully accept their occasional handouts when we meet and though the sibling rivalry filters through, I think we have found ourselves."

The expression and feelings from this woman may be an extreme reaction. Many factors play a part in the reaction of a child placed in this position. The parent's awareness of what may be taking place in the mind of the older child is terribly important. But how can one know what a child is thinking? The temperament of the child is also an influencing factor.

We all know, yet perhaps need to be reminded, that:

1. We have no say in our birth order.

2. We have no say in whether we will be a multiple birth.

3. We have no control over how many siblings we will have in our family.

4. We have no say in who our parents will be: rich, poor, the race, degree of education, the nature of our parents (compassionate, loving, hateful, angry, self-serving, and on and on.)

5. We have no control over the occupation of our parents.

You might say life is a real gamble and some hit the jackpot, others don't. Some are born into comfortable loving homes. Sadly others are born into homes where there is little security and any sign of love within the family is hard to detect.

I mention the above because I think we need to understand a bit about the relationship between the kind of home atmosphere we are born into and how it affects how we are going to respond to our environment.

Helping Siblings Adjust to Twins Entering the Family.

Not only are parents adjusting to having twins in the family—so are siblings. It's important to give each member of the family a chance to get to know these new members on an individual basis. Here are some possible ways this might be accomplished:

1. When the twin children are old enough, it would be wise to see that older siblings get individual time with each twin.

2. Don't be afraid to take one of the twin babies out at a time, along with one sibling, on brief outings, being sure the trips are equal in the number of times and length of duration.

3. No amount of praise is too much to give when an older sibling is assisting in the care of their twin siblings.

4. If there is hired help coming in, it would be wise to have them get to know the older children, and spend a bit of time with them as well as the two new members of the family.

5. Communication is a big key to having happy siblings of twins. Look for ways your single children can express their feelings about having twins in the family.

Talk about positives that have happened since twin children have come to be a part of the family. Also hear when they speak of the negatives, and share open dialogue.

1. We get more company.

2. There are more toys in the house.

3. We get to entertain them.

4. The house seems cluttered.

5. There is a lot more laundry and work.

One mother told me "Our twins arrived totally unexpectedly. Our older girl was unprepared for two. She wanted one girl and got two boys. There was instant hostility. Many temper tantrums (which had been outgrown) returned. She was very jealous and physically hurtful to the twins. But she is very possessive around outsiders and when others ask about her 'babies' she is very proud and wants them to be noticed. Some hostility is gone since she is now five-and-a-half, but she still has tantrums when she thinks she's left out."

Living with twins in a family has got to be a memorable experience for singletons and parents alike. I asked an older sister what she recalled about living with two very identical twins as they were growing up. She wrote, "I remember being shown the new babies and felt awe and joy. I have always felt great love for them and always protective of them, probably because they are younger than I. Along with this I have been very proud to have the privilege of having them for sisters and in my family. I feel all four sisters are happily close to each other. A camp director told me she remembers how close they were at camp. When one cried, the other cried. When one had an earache, they both had an earache."

Siblings and Twins Express Themselves

Over the last fifteen years I've had the privilege of hearing from many siblings of twins. They have told how the addition of twins into their family affected them. Parents of twins have told me how their older and younger children have felt about having twins in the family. What they share with us can help parents of twins be aware of the feelings that are often not expressed by siblings, but are kept inside, only to be expressed by hostile action.

I've written this chapter primarily for two reasons.:

1. To help siblings better understand where the twins in their family are coming from.

2. To help twins better understand how siblings may feel when they live with twins in the family.

What Twins Have to Say to Siblings

1. It was only after we were home and got a bit older that we realized there were two of us. We were not aware that we doubled up on our parents…that we'd take twice as much of their time, and take it away from you.

2. We didn't know we looked so alike we would get most, if not all, of the attention when onlookers saw us.

3. We didn't know two of us would take so much time being cared for that you would not get as much attention as you had been given before we arrived.

4. As we got older we enjoyed our own company with each other so much we didn't spend much time with you. It seemed like we enjoyed the same things. We didn't mean to shut you out of our lives. We are sorry now. We didn't understand. We wish we'd gotten to know you better.

5. We meant no malice when we used to gang up on you. We realize now that two can sometimes carry double power. Two against one really isn't fair.

6. When we got new clothes and you sometimes got hand-me-downs, we didn't realize we got new clothes because we were twins and there had to be two outfits instead of one. (At least that's what we, or our parents thought.)

7. We sometimes didn't think it was fair for you to have your own birthday party and get your own gifts; most of the time we got identical gifts or had to share a gift and card.

What Siblings Have to Say to Twins

1. You made our family famous. We had twins!

2. After you arrived attention was on you instead of us.

3. Forgive us for sometimes feeling jealous when our parents seemed to give you attention that once was ours.

4. We're sorry we sometimes resented you because we were often asked to give our playtime in helping care for you.

5. After your arrival, it seemed we didn't get to have special outings as often as before. Now we realize two more babies take more money and there was less for outside fun like movies and amusement parks.

6. We are sorry now we used to get mad at you for getting into our things: our school work, jewelry, makeup, and our toys.

7. At times it seemed you got more privileges than we,

because there were two of you. Now we understand our folks thought you could look after each other—there being safety in numbers.

Words from Parents of Twins

Following are just a few of hundreds of comments I've heard from parents of twins about the siblings' reactions when twins have been brought into a family. In their remarks you will see in action some of the issues that are included in the feelings expressed from siblings to twins, and twins to siblings.

One mother wrote "Our oldest daughter is fifteen, our twins are twelve, girls, and our youngest daughter is four. Our older daughter resents twins. She has been to counseling for it. She is sometimes very bitter and cruel to them, but they have each other and she really can't hurt them for long. Our youngest is a spoiled brat and a bully. She picks on them and often hurts them, but they love her dearly. Even though they have problems, I think they all love each other very much."

Another told me "Ours are eleven, fifteen, eighteen, and twenty. All of my children have shown a great deal of love to the twins. My oldest son, even though he has always helped with the twins cannot tell them apart. There has been some jealousy from my 11 year old who is closest in age to the twins, and also the only other girl. Most of the time she is very proud of them and likes to show them off to her friends."

This mother said "Our son was two when our twin daughters were born. When I brought them home from the hospital he really didn't mind them. But now they touch his toys and they can walk. He feels hostility and jealousy!"

A mother wrote that she has a daughter, eight, one six, and three-and-a-half year old twin daughters. Of them she wrote, "Our oldest is very protective of the twins and has a deep mothering attitude toward them. Our second child was only two at the birth of the twins. She adapted well and was not jealous of them, but seems to require extra attention now."

"Our son, who was two when the twins were born, was jealous

at first of the attention they received, then he became proud of them after he saw there was no difference in our love for him."

"Older sister (four years older,) wanted to give one away when they were first brought home from the hospital, as she was only expecting to have one sister or brother. Twins were diagnosed five days before their birth."

One mother told me she had a little girl three and a little boy two when she surprised the family by giving birth to twin daughters. She said, "My two singles are close in age to the twins and they are all wonderful together. I have never seen any sign of jealousy."

Another mother wrote that her little daughter was three when twin girls were born, she said, "As a whole she is real good about all the attention the twins get. The only time the jealousy is there is when company comes and they show a lot of attention to the twins.

This mother said,"Our son is two and a half years older than our twin daughters. We see some jealousy. We try hard to include him in the praise, comments, etc. lauded upon the twins, either by friends or strangers."

"We had a little girl, four, and one, twenty-three months, when our twin daughters were born. Our oldest was so excited when we found out we were having twins that she would tell anyone and everyone, 'Guess what my mom is having—twins!' She takes care of them when I need her help. My second hugs and kisses them all the time, and has not shown any signs of dislike, but she is not that much older so to her they're just little babies."

A mother who had a four-year-old girl and a two-year-old girl when twin daughters were born wrote, "Pride was shown by the four year old. We get out of the car and see other people and she tells the people we have twins. The two year old shows much jealousy. She enjoys them but also wants to be a baby. Being only two when they were born and the shock of being replaced by two babies caused much emotional upheaval and also bedwetting."

"Our three-year-old tried to give one or both of the twins away on numerous occasions. Once she offered a friend with twins the same age a trade—one of ours for one of hers. She pointed out to us it's silly for us to have something that looks the same—at least her way we'd have two that look different. My solution to this has been to try to arrange special activities for this daughter—preschool, dancing, etc.—some activity that is only hers."

"My older daughter, who was five when our twin daughters were born, was quite jealous and has remained jealous of all the attention, even if it's negative attention. If I'm yelling at the younger ones, she resents the time I spend directing attention to them," wrote another mother.

One mother said, "Our son was two-and-a-half when our daughters were born. At first it was awe. He understood they were different than his friend's mother who just had one baby, but didn't understand why we got two. Then when the twins were walking it was jealousy and hostility. He is now in school and shows pride in them. His sisters can't wait for him to get out of school; they hug him and he always carries one out to the car."

Another said, "I thought it was doubly difficult for my older son to adjust to the babies coming home. He was four years old and had been the only child. The babies took so much of my time I had little time to spend with my son and husband. And even less time for myself."

One of the greatest safeguards that can be used to lessen the degree of hostility within a family is to encourage members to express their true feelings, both negative and positive. It seems this is best accomplished through communication. Being able to spend individual time with each member of a family would seem the ideal way for this to happen.

Such a requirement may seem a near impossibility when there are many members in the family, but the length is not as important as the individual time spent with each child. Sometimes a little goes a long way. It's just like chocolate, the more the better, but some is better than none.

One-on-one time, eyeball time, I call it, is when I feel two minds really connect. It's a time when you can pretty much be assured that what you are saying is being heard.

Perhaps we should close this chapter with a bit of what I call timely advice to both twins, siblings of twins and parents of twins.

As you think about past experiences, remember that at the time you did the best you could with the understanding and experience you had. This goes for you and for all the members of your family. There is no room for "If only I'd..."

There is the *now!* Aren't we all thankful for *now?* There's no time like the present to express your feeling with your parents, twin, or siblings.

Chapter Nine

Relationship with Spouse

"They didn't know they were marrying both of us."

In this chapter you will read about twins who have happy marriages and twins who have experienced unhappy marriages. You will learn the effects these two kinds of marriages have had upon other family members. We will look deep inside some marriages and hope to see what elements are essential in order to make twin marriages work. We will attempt to find out what it is that erodes a twin's marriage.

Two Husbands—One Wife

Those of you who have read my first book, *We Are Twins, But Who Am I?* are already aware of the strange relationship you will read about here. It sounds so bizarre, yet it tells how two identical twins resolved their concerns about getting married. I hasten to add that I do not condone such a drastic solution; however, I am always made glad when I see a happy family sharing life together in a pleasant atmosphere of congeniality and love.

A feature in a tabloid newspaper printed in May 1989 carried this story of identical twins who shared a wife and happily raised the children of their three-cornered union.

According to the report, twin brothers Art and Bart Stevers are Australian fire fighters who love to play golf, eat pizza and come home to the same pretty redhead named Judy. She is the mother and the twins are the fathers of four children by her.

The twins are satisfied living as one big happy family with their wife, four children and two collies. The mother of the boys, Georgine, said her sons never had any trouble finding girls, but neither of them had ever met someone special enough to settle down with until Judy came along.

Art met her while he was working the midnight shift. She was a new dispatcher. Three weeks later, Art's new girlfriend was transferred to the day shift and met Bart, who reported to his mother a few days later that he had met the woman of his dreams: the dispatcher who used to work nights.

Georgine said she was not surprised by the double attraction. "My boys have always liked the same things," she said.

Far from considering the triangle a threat to their close relationship, Art and Bart decided to share their favorite girl, with her permission. Judy didn't mind and soon the trio moved into her spacious home near Brisbane, Australia.

"We share everything in this house, including love," said Judy, explaining that a practical sleeping arrangement was mapped out in which Judy shared Art's bed three nights a week, then transferred to Bart's bed for three nights. "I don't count who gets the extra day," Judy said. "Neither do they because in the end it all evens out."

Besides sharing the love-making, the twins also share the parental responsibilities of their four children. "We raise them all together as both our children," said Bart, pointing out that there was no way the twins could know who fathered which child. "Since they are all the same genetically, it just doesn't matter," Art said.

Although the Stevers kids take a lot of ribbing at school, they profess to love the unusual life style. "It's like having two dads," said twelve-year-old Lionel.

Though unusual, Art and Bart's connubial sharing demonstrates in the extreme the "couple effect" twins develop between themselves. It is this affinity of feelings, thoughts, likes and dislikes, even sexual attraction to marriage partners, that make the matrimonial unions of twins among the best and the worst.

Marriage, at best, asks that two people mesh different backgrounds, or at least it asks that they attempt to understand the kind of shoes the other has worn prior to marriage. Think, then, of the added dimension when three sets of shoes enter the picture when only two were expected.

What is it in the relationship of identical twins that may cause their hesitation to marry someone other than an identical twin?

1. Many of these twins feel so in tune with one another that their ideas are communicated to their twin even before they express themselves. These twins often finish one another's sentences. It may take a bit of patience to live with a non-twin who hasn't a clue about what a person is going to say until they express themselves.

2. Identical twins often enjoy the same type of activities, same foods, share the same friends, and experience the same physical feelings. They can't say to their non-twin spouse, "You know how I feel," because they don't. And they never will—only their twin will know.

3. There is very often an intense commitment, loyalty and devotion felt by these twins. Many have said to me, "I often have the urge to tell my twin about some news, or event, before I tell my spouse." I must say I was shocked early on in my research when one identical twin told me that if she, her twin and her husband were out in a boat and one was going to drown, she would have to say it was her husband that would have to go.

Fraternal twins, being no more genetically alike than any other siblings, are less likely to be affected by twinship when making a switch from twin to spouse.

Some factors that might enter the twin equation and could affect the marriage are:

1. A strong dependence of one twin upon the other,

sometimes resulting in a transference of dependency from twin to spouse.

2. Feelings of inadequacy within the twin relationship because of a feeling of being 'put-down' or inferior, resulting in a continued low self-esteem.

3. A dominant twin who was always the leader is likely to transfer that dominance over to the spouse.

Anyone about to marry a twin needs to learn all there is to learn about twins. They need to know the difference between identical and fraternal twins. They need to be extremely aware of, and observe, the interaction that takes place between the one they love and the bond that exists between them and their twin. More than once I've been told "I didn't know I was marrying two instead of one."

Not only do you need to get a grasp on the close bond that may, and most often will exist; you need to search deep inside your own thoughts and feelings. You might be wise to ask yourself these questions:

1. Will I be jealous if my spouse spends a great deal of time with their twin?

2. Can I be tolerant of the time spent in long distance phone calls, not to mention the money?

3. Can I accept with humor the times when I may be tricked into thinking I am talking to my wife/husband when it was the other twin?

Jealousy

It is jealousy that is most often the culprit causing problems in a marriage relationship between a twin and spouse.

A woman who had been married to an identical twin for many years wrote me a sad letter. She had learned I was writing a book on twins and hoped I might be able to help her better understand the thinking of twins. She wrote,

"After thirty-three years I am still trying to understand the relationship between those two men. I know there must be a lot of wonderful things about being a twin, however, I also think there are a lot of things that are not so wonderful. I'm saddened and disappointed that my marriage ended in divorce, but I'm even sadder that my ex-husband's relationship with his children takes a back seat to his relationship with his brother. One of my children said one day he hoped his Uncle Tim died first, so he might have some time with his own father. Of course, the kids feel guilty for feeling this way, but I certainly understand their feelings.

"As Ray's wife, I always knew I was at the bottom of his list of priorities. Loyalty to his brother and his brother's family always came before his loyalty to me and our children."

One wonders if communication early on in the marriage might have prevented the divorce.

Understanding the Twin Bond

Over the past several years I have been in close contact with a woman who feels great loneliness and a degree of separation even though she and her twin live in the same town. Her husband is extremely jealous of the time she spends with her twin sister. I was told my book, *We Are Twins, But Who Am I?* is on their coffee table, and they have asked him to read it, but it goes untouched by him. They have told him there is a chapter in the book about twins and marriage, but he is not interested in learning about twins and their feelings.

Spouses of twins can endear themselves to their marriage partners by understanding, or at least by trying to understand, the twin bond and how important it is to their mate. Following are just some of the many comments made to me that support this belief.

"I respect the twin bond an awful lot. I recognize my wife's need to see her twin as frequently as possible and I understand there is a need and love there that goes beyond a husband/wife relationship."

"I feel there's a camaraderie between the twins. While it

doesn't threaten me, I know I need to make allowances for it. For example, what might be secret between a man and a wife is not necessarily secret between a man, a wife and a wife's twin. I think my wife's twin knows me very well because, in a certain way, I am shared with her. I think my wife and her twin use both their lives as twins to validate their lives individually."

One twin said "I think being a twin has affected my married life in that he did not realize what he was getting himself into when he married me! That is to say my twin sister and I are very close (closer than the average sister relationship.) When my twin sister and I would get together (after we were both married) my husband said he tended to feel a little bit 'left out' and didn't totally understand why. Now that we've been married for 25 years he doesn't feel hurt or left out anymore—he just realizes that is the way things are!"

Marrying a twin is different than marrying a singly born child because a twin's background includes:

1. Early conditioning of starting life with a constant companion. Being used to having another with them to share thoughts and express feelings.

2. Someone with whom they learn to give and take and negotiate.

3. Someone with whom they share affection with family members.

4. Another person who understands them. (This seems to apply much more often to the identicals who are genetically alike.)

I asked: "Do you feel being a twin helped you move easily into the marriage relationship, or made it more difficult to move into a marriage relationship?" Their responses were:

"I don't know if twinship had a significant effect on my ability to move into a marriage relationship. I was accustomed to living very closely with someone who knew almost everything about me, but marriage of course is much more intimate. I don't really believe my life as a twin had a big role in marriage preparation, although it did help me develop some personality traits which I believe contribute to a happy marriage."

"I already knew how to share and talk things out with someone close because I grew up with love, understanding and companionship."

"I don't honestly think growing up as a twin had any effect on the beginning of my marriage. I was able to easily form a marriage relationship, although my twin's approval was important. If my twin had not liked my choice of a mate, I'm sure I wouldn't have felt as secure. The only difficulty I remember from this time period was a longing for my twin to also be married. I made special effort to make sure she caught the bouquet at my wedding because it was important to me that she would be married soon after me. When she did not get married in the following years, it was a constant source of concern but that concern had no adverse effect on my marriage."

"It helped me move easily into the marriage relationship because of the one-on-one relation I had with my twin. It was natural for me to worry about my husband, and care about his feelings, as I have and still do with my twin."

"I'm not aware that being a twin had anything significant to do with me establishing my marriage relationship. Perhaps my loyalty to my twin transferred to my loyalty to my husband. I think my strong bond with my twin is a reason why I have such a strong bond with my husband."

"I can remember when my twin announced he was getting married I had some thought of abandonment or separation anxiety. I did not resent this at all. If anything, it rather influenced me to think about marriage myself and I did marry the following year. In some subtle way it meant approbation to enter into a conjugal relationship."

Good communication is vital for twins as they try to explain their feelings to their mates. During the past ten years I have had the privilege of observing the strengthening of the marriage bond between twins and their spouses. Many of them are married to wonderful mates who try to understand what it must be like to have been born a twin. Some have told me they tried to get their spouses to understand the love they have for their twin is different than the love they have for their mate. One twin, who is making real progress in her growth relationship with her twin wrote, "I pray for my selfishness not to get in the way of our understanding." She goes on, "It's all so complicated. Obviously I haven't figured it all out yet."

One male twin asked his wife whether she thought his twinship helped or hindered in their marriage. She wrote, "I feel that my husband's relationship with his twin has helped him move into a marriage relationship smoothly in most ways. He is a very tenderhearted person, and it is not usually difficult for him to discuss his feelings, and to express himself. Perhaps being a twin, and having a close relationship with his brother has made this easier."

Another wrote, "Yes, I think being a twin helped me in my marriage. It helped me relate with my husband for the closeness and friendship one needs as a wife and husband."

"Since I was used to thinking in terms of 'we' for everything it was probably easier to move into a marriage relationship. I was always used to sharing everything; time, energy, ideas, things. I just continued to do so; however, many years later I realized I did not develop myself individually, which is related to having been a twin. It was hard for me to know what 'I liked,' what 'I wanted,' 'How I felt.' Those 'I' phrases were not a part of my thinking. It has only been in the later years of my life that I became just me. This has, of course, had a negative impact on my own development and therefore the marriage relationship."

"My husband does admit to a streak of jealousy that has diminished with the years...but still pops out every now and then. When it shows...we tease him about it...and that seems to take care of the problem. It we weren't all aware of it and couldn't talk about it, it might be a problem. We have all managed to deal with it openly...and that helps!"

The twin just quoted is an excellent example of the power that communication holds. Surely, many of the divorces that take place, come about because of the lack of understanding of the importance of communication, or the failure to realize that therein lies the solution to many problems. Problems that, could they be solved, would save husbands and wives and children inestimable pain and sorrow.

Twin's Advice to Anyone Marrying a Twin

In my initial questionnaire to twins I did not research twins and marriage, but after receiving several hundred responses, I knew I must do further research on twins and marriage. Following are just some of the many comments made to me from twins from ages 20-70 as they reflected back upon their married life.

"I always thought in terms of 'we' rather than 'I'. In essence, I divorced my brother when I married my wife."

"Be patient with your spouse, for it may be hard for him to understand the feelings of twins. Keep communicating and communicating, because if you don't there will be problems. I know," she observed, "for somewhere along the way in our relationship we stopped communicating and were divorced after thirteen years of marriage and three beautiful children. He really had problems with the twin in my life."

"If the twins are close, I would advise the husband or wife to be aware of the fact that there is a very special close relationship. I would hope they would all get along because it will mean a lot if the family get-togethers can be happy and joyful.

"There is a very special bonding between identical twins. They are soul mates—another self. They share secret jokes, confidences, and a perfect companionship. You may feel hurt and shut out when you cannot penetrate the closeness of their affection for each other.

"You could feel jealous, threatened and very competitive toward the other spouse, if the other twin is married.

"The twins should both have a great capacity for loving you and your children since there has always been this loving bond between the twins themselves.

"You could either like, or you could resent all the attention the twins get when they are together. Two such identical beings are sometimes a fascination to others. Twins are very protective of each other, so if you hurt one's feelings, the other twin will probably feel hurt also.

"When twins play games together it probably won't matter to them which twin wins, for if your twin wins, it is like winning yourself.

"Twins can pretty well be expected to stand together on the same side in any argument, even against you."

Thus ends a rather long message from an identical twin.

Twins who grow up in a non-threatening and happy homelife are much more likely to make better partners than twins who fought from birth on to be heard above their twin. Often twins are going to seek what they did not have in their childhood— perhaps a chance to be heard (if they were in the shadow of the other), or perhaps they will expect their spouse to take the lead because that is what they always knew in the twin relationship as they were growing up.

Quantary Marriages—When Twins Marry Twins

Some twins, most always identical twins, opt for not marrying unless they can marry another pair of twins. I put this question to one set of identical men. They had planned to postpone marriage until they could find the right set of twins to marry, but they are now married. I think you will find their responses interesting.

1. Question: **What do you feel are the advantages of twins marrying twins?**

    Twin No 1 - "I feel there ought to be teamwork among the four people and that constant understanding in the relationship will make it work. Thus the transition of being single into being married will be much easier."

    Twin No. 2 - "One advantage of marrying twins is that you are not losing the twin bond totally. You are just replacing it with another person who already understands what it means to be a twin."

2. Question: **What do you feel causes twins marrying non-twins to break up?**

> Twin No. 1: "One major factor is that the non-twin is jealous of the spouse's twin. He or she does not understand the twin bond and begins to feel left out. You have to realize that if you marry a twin you should not try to replace the twin who remains single."

> Twin No. 2: "I believe the real reason marriages break up is that the spouse who is marrying the twin does not understand the twin bond and thus becomes jealous. The spouse tries to replace the twin who is now separated from his/her twin, and he learns this cannot be done.

> "Lack of communication is another cause for the marriage to break up. Open communication is the key if this kind of relationship is to work. If the non-twin is negative about anything in the twin relationship and says nothing about it, they will run into problems during their relationship as husband and wife."

3. Question: **What preventive measures do you feel can be taken by twins and their twin spouses prior to marriage?**

> Twin No. 1: "All parties must realize that in addition to the twin relationship, there have to be unwritten rules made by the couples regarding privacy which must prevail in the relationship between husband and wife. A twin needs time alone with a spouse. Going out as a foursome is great and some even enjoy the attention paid them, but each couple must have time alone without the other couple. This may mean living far enough apart as they would if they lived in two apartments in the same building or in side-by-side duplexes. You can still be close, but you do need time apart from one another."

> Twin No. 2: "I agree with my brother's thoughts on this subject. Privacy must be there along with companionship. If you have a balance here, you won't have any major

difficulty." Also, each twin has personality traits different from the other. If each twin knows the limitations and strengths of the other twin, then there will be a good chance this understanding will carry over into the relationship they have with their spouse. The twins have to understand and respect their spouses' feelings and help them overcome any jealousy they may have. Teamwork is the essential ingredient in conquering all odds."

Not Marrying Just One, But Two

As you will see by looking at the questionnaire at the back of the book, I did not include any questions dealing with marriage and twins. It was only after I received several hundred of the completed questionnaires that I recognized the need to learn what it is about twinship that often results in heavy conflict. It behooves anyone about to marry a twin to learn all they can about their mate to be, and be as knowledgeable about twins as possible, especially the relationship between the fiance and their twin. Some spouses of twins have told me it is almost like "not marrying just one, but two."

In doing more research regarding marriage and twins, I tried to get responses from spouses of twins. I asked Karen to put this question to her husband, "How is it being married to a twin?" His answer to her was, "I got the best one." Karen went on, "He thinks I am the best looking, most talented and have a better personality. Rachel's husband thinks the same thing about her. Rachel and I know they are both right. I'm sure they didn't know they were marrying both of us. But, fortunately, we are all good friends and get along beautifully. Our husbands are friends...our daughters are friends... and of course, Rachel and I are twins."

Chapter Ten

Relationship with Grandparents

It is with firsthand experience that I tell what it's like to be a grandparent of twins, for I am one of them. Had it not been for our son and his wife blessing us with twin grandsons, I would never have found myself writing books about twins.

All our friends were bragging about the births of their grandchildren. My husband and I were bemoaning the fact that it looked like we would never have them. Our son had been married for seven years, which seemed long enough for us to have to wait for the next generation. With your indulgence may I share my introduction to learning twins were in utero.

My husband was not home. A phone call from our son set me into orbit when I heard his words, "The doctor told us today we are going to have twins."

I let out a "Yippee!!" Our two dogs, Buster and Cindy, who were always my shadows, wondered what had happened.

Since I would be in bed before my husband came home, I hurriedly scribbled out a bit of verse for him and left it by the phone.

What News, What News!
I can't believe it's true.
What we once thought was one,
Has now jumped to two.

I can't stand up,
And I can't sit down.
And there's no one around
But the the dogs and me—
And they think I act a
Bit funny.

Joyous news is all I can say
What a wonderful way to end a day.

As I look back upon it all now I wonder why I didn't suspect the possibilities of twins since I was born into a family with two sets of twins—all fraternal—and this type of twin being hereditary.

My twin grandsons are now fifteen years old and I've found that observing them from day one until now has been a joyful experience. I believe I can honestly say I have viewed them as their own selves first and as twins second, all these years. Could this stem from my being a twin? Possibly.

Being a twin, I believe, may have been of help to me as I developed a relationship with each of them. I've always cherished the times when I've been able to spend time with them together and separately.

As toddlers they were almost always together, so I found both my hips being warmed as I read them their favorite story books. As we played games we noticed that each of us had different skills. I pointed out the differences in each of us, stating that we're all born with our own talents. Never did I pit the ability of one against the other.

Grandparents play a very special role for children; no one

can take their place, for it is they who can tell them what their parents were like when they were little boys and girls.

There are rich rewards for grandparents who establish a warm relationship with each of their grandchildren.

My travels have put me in contact with many adult twins. They have shared with me how they felt enriched or diminished by the way they were treated by their grandparents as children.

One identical twin wrote, "I missed out on a one-to-one parent/child encounter. I do not recall separate conversations with either parent—except when I was home sick. I did have glimpses of this experience with my grandmother."

How can grandparents establish a warm and loving relationship with each of their twin grandchildren? Here are few tips that will point you in the right direction:

1.   First, and foremost, learn the name of each child and attach it to the right child. This may sound absurd, but it isn't. Try to avoid referring to them, or speaking of them as "The boys, the girls, the twins." So many of the people who took part in my research said they were often lumped together as a 'unit' when they were addressed. Most of them wished people had called them by their given name.

2.   Think of each of them as unique, separate people, for that is exactly what they are. It takes real awareness to be able to do this, especially when a quick glance at them tells you they look the same.

3.   Nip in the bud any tendency to compare them. Is this an easy assignment? No. But the rewards you will be given in return will be worth all the effort. If you are fortunate enough to know twins are on the way, you can prepare yourself mentally for how you are going to view and treat them. They are going to have enough comparison from onlookers who are not aware of how painful comparison can be to twins. You can let it be known that you were blessed with two grandchildren at once. It isn't bragging to add, "And I find each of them so interesting in their own way." That comment gives a subtle message that even though they are twins, they are unique, and that is the way you see and treat them.

4.   Make the effort to spend individual time with each of

them. When you are with them together, it is easy to direct one question to both. The answer will most often come in unison and you may not get the same answer if they were asked individually. Twins often color the thoughts of the other. When you have special time with them and make eye-to-eye contact, they know you are giving them your undivided attention.

Direct your question to them individually. One question put to both of them fosters one usually taking the lead in responding. It's amazing how fast a pattern of response can develop. "This is my twin sister, but she doesn't talk very much!" The reason very often may be—because the one twin always jumps the gun and answers for both.

5.   Choose the right gift for each of them. That is most easily accomplished when you know the interests of each. Getting to know each of your grandchildren well—his or her likes and dislikes—will go a long way in helping you make the right choice. Some twins will be happy only when the gifts are the same. Some will want them to be different.

6.   Treat them to special events or visits with you, individually. You not only treat them and yourself, but their parents as well. It's good for twin children to be able to say 'Hello' and 'goodbye' to one another since they usually spend so much time together. Your taking one gives their parents a chance to spend special time with the other. Each child has a chance to have a captive audience, and where is the person that does not like that? At least once in a while.

7.   Occasionally, have your picture taken with each of them individually. You won't have to work at having many pictures of them with you together, but it may take some planning to see that you have some photos taken with them individually.

8.   Make photograph albums for each of them. I started doing this immediately after my twin grandsons were born and I'm well into their second albums. When they were small, they loved to look at their own photographs—someday they will mean a lot to them.

9.   Make tape recordings of each as they develop. Let each have his own tape on which they sing their little songs, and say

their nursery rhymes. Tape recorders can capture the special words they say in a school play. I cherish the tapes where I have both of them in interaction with one another. These tapes will remind me of the specialness that my twin grandchildren have by being born twins—with a built-in playmate!

10.   If space in your home allows, see that each has a shelf where he can have his own coloring books, crayons and special toys. Let them know their things are for sharing but the things on their shelf are theirs—to keep orderly or messy. This is a subtle way to let your grandchildren know that you recognize them as individuals.

These tips are stepping stones in building a solid base for unity and communication between you and each of your grandchildren.

Perhaps you can come up with other ways that will help you establish a close bond with each child. Can you think of a greater compliment than when your grandchild says to you, "I want to spend the night with you."

I am reminded of a scene that took place recently as we celebrated the birthday of our oldest granddaughter. As she was opening her gifts, one of our younger granddaughters came to me and asked, "Did you bring me anything?" I looked at her and said, "Yes, I brought you 'me.' She thought a second and then said, "Oh," accompanied by a big smile.

Besides having twin grandsons, my husband and I have three little granddaughters. From the time they were toddlers we have had them take turns spending a day and night with us. They keep track of 'their time' with not just me, but with us. It's a special time for them and a special time for us.

The above thought leads me to close with this special reminder. Often it is the grandmother who initiates the special event, or the suggestion to have a grandchild visit. Grandmothers are very important, but just as important are grandfathers. Each plays a special role in the lives of their grandchildren. Grandfathers, please forgive me for suggesting that grandfathers may not appear to be as involved in the lives of your grandchildren as are grandmothers. I couldn't resist mentioning it just in case there might be one or two grandfathers who might be missing out on the special experience of grandparenting twins or non-twins.

If there are other children in the family with twins, I beg you to be aware of the reinforcement that siblings of twins need in order for them to feel just as important as their twin siblings.

Chapter Eleven

Relationship with Family After Loss of Twin

Parents and Siblings

To lose any member of one's family is an event for which none of us are ever prepared. With such loss each member of the family is often in a state of shock. For a twin, they have lost a member of their family, but they have also lost their twin. Parents are grieving, siblings are grieving—each in his own way. At this time each is consumed with his own grief. It is understandable when members fail to reach out to comfort other members of their family.

This is a time when family members need to join forces and gather round one another. It is a time for sharing thoughts and feelings; for showing expressions of love, perhaps in ways they are not usually shown.

As I have talked with grieving twinless twins, and their parents, I have found the families that make it easier to work through the grieving process, are those where there remains open communication between all members. I have found those family members who are able to express themselves, and know they are being heard and understood, are the ones who are better able to accept the loss and begin the healing process.

It is often difficult for parents to understand the intense loss a twin may experience when they lose their twin. The surviving twin may be told "We hurt as much as you do." The twin may feel anger over the seeming lack of understanding of their parents. Sometimes parents will want to cease mentioning the twin who no longer lives. I have found that most twins want to talk about their twin and they want others to listen; they want to keep the memory of their twin alive.

A person who has lost their twin may feel guilt over not giving support to their parents, who are also grieving.

A woman who recently lost her twin to suicide wrote, "My parents are grief-stricken, but I'm in so much pain I find it hard to try to help them with their pain."

If the parents have stressed too strongly the specialness of 'twins, the twin survivor may feel less loved since there is now only *one*.

The relationship of the twinless twin and the parents may change. The parents, knowing they lost one and could lose another, may become overprotective. If hovering of the parents becomes too intense, it may cause a greater dependency or blatant lack of safety for self.

In one of my questionnaires I asked twins if they had ever given thought to the time when they could lose their twin to death. Some flatly said they didn't want to think about it as it was too hard for them to imagine. Others had talked with their twin about such a possibility, some even mentioning they would join each other in Heaven.

In my first book I talked about an identical twin who lost her twin in a car accident. She shares with us some comments. "I remember thinking once, before my twin died, could I live without her?' My answer was *'No way!'* Well, I have. It's a struggle every day. For the longest time, I expected her to show up. I know the next time I see her, we'll be in Heaven.

"I've had a real struggle inside with my feelings. I'll never let anyone get as close to me as she was. No one could take her place no matter how they tried. Just as I could never love anyone like I did her. In a way I feel I loved her too much. It hurts (still hurts) too much. I found myself holding back love from my family. I wouldn't give my 'all.' I never want to hurt that bad again. I was real reserved with my elderly father. I went to the cemetery one day, and sitting there, I realized if I could do it over again I would give her all the love I gave and probably more."

To update you on this identical woman, I talked with her recently, and she told me she finds great pleasure working in her garden since she and her father spent many hours in that activity after the death of her twin.

This woman's reaction to the loss of her sister expresses what other twinless twins have told me. They feel they will never get as close to another person because of the intense feeling of loss when death occurs.

You have read in other chapters of this book about the extreme closeness of some twins. Often it is the closeness that results in the exclusion of other members of the family.

I recall so vividly my contact with a mother of identical twin girls in their early 20s. She had almost felt locked out from their lives at times because of their intense devotion to one another. When one of the girls died very suddenly, there seemed to appear an impenetrable wall between her and her daughter. She yearned so intensely to comfort her daughter, yet felt a distance she did not know how to close.

I suggested she put her feelings on the loss of her daughter on paper and send them to me. With great care she searched her soul and felt relief in her expressions. Prior to sending the letter to me she decided to send it to her daughter for comments. The response from her daughter's reading began the healing process for both of them. The daughter had not realized how her mother was feeling. As a result of her mother's exposure of how she felt, the daughter then opened a floodgate of thoughts which she shared with her mother.

Very often twins who have kept their lives so closely knit have not expanded their relationships with others. With the loss of their twin it behooves them to extend themselves and reach out to others as they build a network of additional friends.

It is always good when each member of the family can assist the other in resolving the trauma that is felt after a family member has died. There can be resentment on the part of a twin who feels their parents have not helped them go through the various stages of grief.

Children need to be able to express themselves in whatever manner is healing to them. A child or twin who is not given the opportunity to show grief, or who is stifled when trying to express feelings may, at the time, or at a later date, feel hostility toward parents who did not appear to listen or empathize with them.

Since it is impossible for a non-twin to understand twin loss, it is extremely helpful if a twin support group is available. Happily I can say there is now some help out there for twinless twins. This could not have been said a decade or so ago. You will find mention of these support groups listed under Resources.

Steps Toward Healing

I have just returned from the third Twinless Twins Conference was held in Fort Wayne, Indiana. Many twinless twins were there from all over the United States. As I observed these twins who were in the process of adjusting to a life without their twin, I was again made aware of the tremendous support that comes from interracting with others who have experienced similar loss.

As a twin researcher I take every opportunity I can to learn new ways to help twins who are grieving. This conference was no exception. I asked twinless participants to respond to several questions. What they shared with me, I believe, will be of interest and of help to you.

The first question asked was, "What has helped you most in your recovery?"

Here are some of their responses:

1 "Finally getting beyond myself and reaching out to, and being open to other twinless twins."

2. "My faith, my dear husband, and my doctor (without

medications). My husband was very understanding because he knew my twin and I were very close."

3. This comment from an opposite sex twin: "My brother's friends, keeping very busy, cherishing his possessions/pictures and placing them prominently in my home."

4. "I had years of therapy with a therapist who has twins and understands twinning. What really changed my life was the first Twinless Twins Conference I attended. I met with others who spoke the same language and really understood. They were so supportive."

5. "I began to recover from the loss of my twin when I began to believe that God takes you when He decides it is time for you to go. Up to that time, I felt guilt-ridden since I was unable to prevent her death.

6. "It was a great comfort to me, knowing that we loved each other greatly while she was alive. It also helped me to know I did the very best for her that I knew how. Helping others has also helped me in my recovery."

The second question asked was "What advice would you offer other twins who have experienced the loss of their twin?" They responded by saying:

1. "Reach out to other twinless twins. Do things to help others. Do things that honor your twin."

2. "I would tell them that life will go on but your life will be changed. Keep going—don't give up. Do experience your anger, sadness, fear, and rage at the world. Do not deny your feelings and don't let others diminish what you feel."

3. "Hang in there. Turn to the Lord. Ask for His strength and He will see you through the rough times."

4. "Be patient with yourself. Seek out other twinless twins. It helps to know you are not going out of your mind."

5. "Talk and talk and talk about your twin. If your family and friends don't want to listen, call any twinless twin! Never set a time limit to grieve. Also, realize that other twinless twins feel this loss every minute of their lives."

6. "It has helped me to have a picture of my twin on my desk at work. Seeing the picture reminds me of the fun and laughter we shared and I think about the day when we will be together again."

The third question asked was, "What would you say to family members?"

They responded by saying:

1. "We are sorry we don't feel your pain because we are so deep into our own loss and numbness. We ask their understanding of our now having to develop our identity as a twinless twin; in a sense we have to become a new person."

2. "Try to understand the pain we have due to the loss of our twin."

3. "Don't insist on birthdays being a reason to celebrate— at least not for the first few years."

4. "Try to understand what we are going through. (I know this is impossible if you are not a twin.)"

5. "Understand that twinless twins have a very special loss. Don't compare your loss to theirs. It's not a contest. Talk about the deceased twin. Read all the material on twin loss."

6. "Let us know you are there to share our feelings and loss and that you are there for us in whatever capacity would help. To assure us that we are not alone, but that we all share in the loss."

If your twin had qualities you admired, try to incorporate them in your life. Develop them within yourself, keeping in mind that you are a vessel through which they might live.

Continue to have a purpose in life. Ask God for direction. He promises to give guidance. Believe that He will lead you. Even if you are a skeptic, be willing to put his promises to a test and work with Him and let Him work through you. Prayer works wonders to those who believe.

You recall reading about Roland and Richard Marshall in the identical men chapter. These men and their wives faced the inevitability of their deaths and took steps to make it easier for their families in the event of a loss. I'm sure their decision to do this also gave them comfort in knowing that someday they would all be placed together. They are the ones who decided to be cremated. They selected a beautiful Mausoleum overlooking the north shore of Lake Washington.

I contacted these men in early November, 1995, to get an update on their lives and their relationship during retirement years. Shortly after Richard wrote me, he suffered a massive heart attack. With Roland and Richard's wives' permission, I have included a letter I received from them.

I chose to close this chapter with the letters from Richard and Roland because through their letters you cannot help but sense the love and devotion these men had for each other and their families. Both of these men recognized their mortality and took steps to make it easier for them after they would no longer be together on earth. What they share may help some of you as you look at your life and plan for the future.

A Tribute to Richard and Roland Marshall

Roland sent me this letter in December of 1996.

Dear Betty Jean,

It is with deep sorrow and a feeling of great loss that I have to tell you of Richard's sudden death on November 30, 1995.

Normally, Richard drove a small bus and sometimes a

specially equipped van on Tuesday and Thursdays for Emerald Heights Retirement Community in Redmond, Washington. He would take members to doctors' appointments at various Hospitals and Clinics in the Bellevue/Seattle area. On Wednesday night the 29th, Richard received a call not to report to work on Thursday until 11 am.

This delay worked out well, for Wednesday night Richard's son Don slept overnight at their house because of the flooded conditions and he could not get home with many roads closed. Richard got up early and fixed their breakfast in the morning before Don left for work.

After Don left, Richard sat in the family room and read a passage from his Bible, Psalms 26. It is Richard's habit after studying a passage to take a pencil and jot down, on the side of the page, the date of study. Richard wrote 11/30/9... Before he could add the '5' his wife, Shirley, said Richard raised both hands over his head and did not respond. She immediately called 911 and five AID people arrived within minutes. The Aid Medics tried for thirty minutes to get Richard's heart rhythm to stabilize and even used the shock treatment to no avail. Then they took him to the local hospital and he was declared dead. Later an autopsy showed Richard suffered a massive heart attack. Prior to this he had never had any known heart problems.

Within the past few years we decided we would like to be cremated in the event of death. In 1991 we located a beautiful Mausoleum in Acacia Memorial Park overlooking the north shore of Lake Washington. At that time we invited Richard and Shirley to look at the facility with us. We decided on two Columbarium spaces side by side. (We called these niches our small Condos.) When it came time to figure out which family would take the left or right space, my wife, Lausanne, suggested that since Roland is left-handed, we take the left space and Richard and Shirley take the right space. We all agreed to that arrangement. Little did we realize that any of these Condo's would be occupied so soon. Needless to say, all of Richard's children and grandchildren were very pleased that both of our families had taken this step four years ago.

After a private committal service at the Columbarium Wednesday morning, we attended the Memorial Service and Celebration of Richard's life at one pm at the First Presbyterian Church of Bellevue. There were 400 people at the service.

The Service was truly a beautiful one with an outpouring of love from those who shared personal experiences as they interacted with Richard in the twenty years he has been a member of the church. Many people from Emerald Heights Retirement Community also spoke.

When the Minister introduced me as the last speaker, he said I was a twin-twin, in that, "they not only look alike and talk alike, but act alike." My purpose was twofold; first, to explain about the special bond that develops for life with twins, and second, to share some twin experiences we had over the years. I mentioned that our Mother always dressed us alike and that I distinctly remembered the first day of school and how we were dressed in a white shirt, tie, knickers, and new brown shoes.

I also pointed out, since we took a Civilian Pilot Training Course in College, we were required to join either the Army or Navy Air Corp immediately, in the event of a war. With Pearl Harbor on December 7, 1941, Richard and I graduated in May 1942 and joined the Navy in June 1942. I explained that when we went to Pre-Flight School in Chapel, North Carolina, the Navy, just like our Mother, insisted we dress alike. However, that didn't bother us since we had been doing that for years. The audible response from these remarks was heartwarming.

The day after Richard's death, his wife, Shirley, gave me Richard's copy of his recent letter to you. I made a copy for myself to study. I am so thankful Richard wrote these six pages of our twin experiences before his sudden death. In the meantime, I had jotted down some notes in preparing to write you. However, since Richard covered in more detail all of the items I intended to mention plus several more, I agree with his remarks and couldn't add any further significant details.

I will always cherish Richard's final letter to you just before he passed away. We had a wonderful 73 years together before Richard was called to be with the Lord. I feel right now that half of my life has departed. I know in my heart that one day we will be together again.

Most sincerely,
Roland Marshall

What follows is the letter Richard wrote me shortly before his death,

Richard A. Marshall
Born 9/15/22
Twin to Roland Marshall

Unexpected

We were not born in a hospital but at the family home, which was common in those days. After Roland was born, Dr. Barnes cleaned up, etc., presented his bill and was paid. Just before he left, Mother said she thought she felt something else was happening. Forty minutes after the first birth, I was born feet first with difficulty.

Almost Died in Maine

Dad had a summer home on Bustins Island three miles off So. Freeport, Maine. Dad was cleaning fish at the water level. Maine has a very rocky coast. I tripped on the top step, fell about seven feet, landed on my head, knocked unconscious, and slipped into the ocean. Dad heard a splash and when he investigated the noise area, he saw some clothes under the seaweed. Needless to say, he saved my life at age five. The impact had damaged the neck cords and I couldn't turn my neck freely for a year needing osteopathic treatments each day until I went to school. I know now God had plans for my young life.

March 23, 1940 Auto Accident

Roland and I worked hard all summer of our Junior year in high school and saved $900 and bought a brand new Ford. On March 23rd, I was driving across a blind railroad crossing in Lexington. The big auto repair shop building was only nine feet from the railroad tracks. The signal lights were not operating and the alarm bell had been inactivated.

Needless to say, the steam-engine type of train hit me at the right front wheel, broke my engine, spun the car around and sheared off the rear, threw the car up against a tree 180 degrees from my original position. Part of the piston of the train came through my right hand door.

When the car hit the tree I was thrown out of the right door. I found myself standing up in the street with a left front tooth in my hand. Injuries were a broken nose between the eyes, facial cuts and other bruises. A police car had been going by the end of the street just as it happened—they rushed me two miles to my family doctor. Again, God had plans for my life. An interesting note: the Conductor of that train had learned his business from my Mother's Father, who had been Head Conductor on the train for forty years.

Teen Age Years

We lived in a big colonial home in a nice area of the historical town of Lexington, Massachussetts. We had our own bedrooms. Normally we had clothes alike because we enjoyed the same things. I would come down to breakfast dressed exactly as Roland and I hadn't known what he was going to wear that day. This happened many times.

When Mother would call us to come into the house, she would call us 'brother' because she couldn't tell us apart. We were both six feet tall and weighed the same.

In high school we had five sets of twins. The older one in each set was left-handed.

College Years

Because of an impending war we went to a two-year junior college to major in Business Administration and to complete it prior to going into the Service.

Before we were born we were 'womb-mates' but in college we were 'room-mates.'

During examinations in a big gymnasium I didn't know where Roland was sitting. We were often accused of cheating because we'd miss the same questions.

One evening I had a date with a girl and we drove off campus and went downtown. It was exam week and I knew Roland was at the dormitory studying. I made an excuse and said I had to go back to the dormitory for something. I never went back to the date — Roland went for me while I studied for the exam. The girl never knew the difference.

After Pearl Harbor hit on December 7th, we signed up for Civil Pilot Training. After graduation, we both joined the Navy to become aviators. We were sworn in about the time of the launching of the new Aircraft Carrier *Lexington*—as we were natives of the town of Lexington where the Revolutionary War was started.

At college graduation we received a joint trophy for highest scholastic achievement, the first time it was awarded to twins.

Portland, Oregon

In 1938, as teenagers, we went with our folks from Boston to San Francisco to a Rotary International Convention. There were lots of young people, including many sets of twins.

As we left San Francisco, Roland looked bad and didn't feel well. During the night he was doubled-up with pain due to a ruptured appendicitis. The three-engine train was stopped in the mountains to telegraph ahead to the hospital in Portland to arrange for an emergency operation. As soon as the train was pulled into the station he was rushed by ambulance to the hospital.

His life was saved because the fluid from the broken appendix was held in a pocket. Fortunately it was not in the normal position. Because of other complications we had to stay one month in a Portland hotel. The Portland Rotary Club was very gracious.

While he was being operated on I took a bus trip with lots of Rotarians to Bonneville Dam. All day I had sympathy pains.

Naval Pilot Training

We went through primary flight training at Memphis, Tenn. During social times we would be with lots of Cadet and local girls, One evening we decided to switch dates without saying anything. The girls never knew the difference but the guys kept laughing a little.

At Corpus Christi, Texas, we were in advanced training. When we were just learning to fly the PBY's—a twin engine seaplane, I used to fly each time it said 'Marshall' on the flight schedule. When Roland finally took his first flight the flight instructor said 'OK, Cadet, taxi it out and prepare for takeoff. Roland said, "Sorry, Sir, this is the first time I've ever been in this plane." He explained that he was my twin brother.

Finally, one day when we were both scheduled to solo separately we decided to see the Commanding Officer and get permission to solo together. It took some talking but we made it. We told him we were going to show the other how well we could fly, etc. Permission granted—it was fun.

During World War II we were supposed to be the first set of twins to receive our Wings and commission as Ensigns at Corpus Christi, Texas. Guess what? The government sent his papers through seven days before mine. He got his Wings first and had to say "Goodbye." Sometime in life this had to happen!!

Tours of Duty

My tour of duty was in the South Atlantic, out of Brazil, chasing German submarines and escorting troop transports for the invasion of Italy, etc. I became a Patrol Plane Commander with my own crew flying the PBM seaplane—we had a crew of about eighteen. We had a 90 million candlepower light under our right wing to make night attacks on submarines.

After a year and a half I took a rest leave to come to the States and get engaged. When I returned thirty days later I learned that my plane and my entire crew had crashed while making a night attack on a German submarine in the mid-Atlantic ocean. Not even a piece of the plane was ever found. After the War a confirmation came from the Germans.

Roland went to the Pacific with a Patrol Squadron of Navy Privateers - like the B24 but with a big single tail. While he was on a rest leave in Australia, one third of his Squadron was destroyed. Had we gotten commissioned together I might have been in that "third." God works in mysterious ways.

One day in Aratu, Brazil, I was instructing a new pilot, assigned to our Squadron, on how to land at night in a particular area of water. While we were at 300 feet, all of a sudden the plane went into an uncontrolled dive and crashed and was demolished. Fortunately no one was seriously hurt. We were rescued. Months later it was learned that plane had crashed on takeoff on the Amazon River in Natal, Brazil. The wing had been damaged, causing the plane to stall at a normally "safe" speed.

Roland stayed in the Navy twenty-six years and also saw action in Korea and Vietnam. While he was instructing French students at Corpus Christi, Texas, in a big four-engine land-type plane, an engine exploded and caused a fire in the left wing. Since there was no way to extinguish the fire he decided to "crash-land" on the water with the wheels up. His experience in flying seaplanes as a Cadet was invaluable on his approach. When the plane sank it put out the fire. No one was badly injured and they were rescued. Later after the plane was recovered and the engine area was examined, a Navy Captain from Washington, DC, told him that another minute in the air the fire would have penetrated the fire-wall and the plane would have exploded in midair. He complimented Roland for his quick judgement to ditch and save all onboard. His wife had delivered a baby girl, number three, a week before in New Hampshire. I was a salesman in the Boston area when I heard this story on the car radio as I was driving around. In my heart I knew that was Roland. It was confirmed when Roland telephoned Mother and Dad in New Hampshire that evening and Dad called me. God works in mysterious ways!

After the War, we were all living with the folks until we each bought a house in Lexington, Massachussetts. Roland and I came into the kitchen together where our wives were preparing a meal. My wife, Shirley, put her arms around Roland and kissed him thinking it was me. She let out a little scream when she recognized the mistake. Such is life.

Roland was called back into the Navy for the Korean conflict and stayed in for a total of twenty-six years. He had purchased a home in Mountain View, CA and owned it for thirty years. He rented it while he moved his family as he was transferred to overseas duty, etc. After he retired from the Navy he again lived in California while I lived on the East Coast. Often I would telephone him and ask him how his *left* knee felt, or some other problem. He would always wonder how I knew something hurt. I knew because my *right* knee hurt.

A Seattle Wedding

While Roland was on a tour of duty at Pearl Harbor in Hawaii, his daughter was finishing college at the University of Washington. After graduation his oldest daughter, Jeanne, was married at the Chapel at University Presbyterian Church in Seattle. Roland couldn't give the bride away personally as he was recovering from a back operation in Hawaii.

During that time I was living in Westfield, New Jersey. My Mother and I flew to Seattle for the big event. I was part of the wedding party and gave the bride away. Most of the people there did not realize I wasn't the Father of the bride. We still laugh about it today. Roland had two other daughters that he did give away in marriage later.

Sand Point Naval Air Station

Roland was Executive Officer (second in command) for three years at this facility. When I came out from New York City on business in Seattle for the first time I stayed with Roland and his family.

Someone threw a big party at their home for the Commanding Officer and lots of Navy people. We happened to arrive a little late. I told Roland to stay up in the kitchen and I walked down to the stairs with Lausanne. The Captain introduced us to all of his friends and never knew I wasn't Roland until Roland finally came down the stairs. It was fun "pulling that off." Twenty years later his Captain said to me at another party "I'll never forget that trick you and Roland played on me years ago."

Sales Career

I was in sales and sales management with Allied Chemical. After twenty-three years at age forty-nine I lost my job while I was in the main office in New York City. Finally after a year I got a sales position in Greenwich, Connecticut. I commuted three hours each day from Westfield, NJ. Also traveled the whole country for the firm. After a year and a half our daughter had her first son in Kirkland, Washington. We came out to see him and I decided to get a one way ticket to the Seattle area. It took me about three days to get a good sales job with a chemical company in Kirkland. I was assigned to travel all of Oregon. Before I could buy a house there I was asked to be their Sales Manager at the main plant in Kirkland. In May 1971, Shirley and I moved to Bellevue, Washington.

When our daughter had her second birth it was identical twin girls who are now 18 years old. They have been a real joy.

About twelve years ago, Roland and Lausanne moved to a nice home in Mill Creek, Washington. Finally after a lifetime of being separated we were able to spend lots of time together. For several years our son, Dick, used to live around the block from Roland. One summer I helped to paint their house. Dick's younger son, Kevin, was only about four years old. He kept calling me Roland because he had seen Roland many more times than me. Dick explained that I was 'Grandpa.' Kevin was confused. Finally Kevin told his Mother that 'Grandpa' was the same but 'Nana' changes. That was a good observation.

Donald's Family

Don and Susie live in Duvall, Washington and have two daughters, Tia and Maile, who are fourteen and twelve, respectively. Nine years ago they flew to Haiti and adopted black twins from an orphanage about 150 miles out of Port-au-Prince. Their Mother had died during childbirth and the Father put them in the orphanage as he couldn't take care of them, etc. All arrangements were made through a Church that worked with the government. The twins were less than a year old.

The day they all arrived to fly to the United States there was an uprising and lots of people were killed, etc. It was a very traumatic time for them as they were hidden in a basement of a Mission House for days. They were finally able to get out on the first Eastern Airlines that go into Port-au-Prince.

Kasey and Kenya are lovely second graders now and growing up fast. There is such love in that family. They are all strong Christians. It has been a real joy to watch them grow up and develop their personalities.

When our kids and the nine grandchildren (ages nine to twenty-one) all get together at our house for Thanksgiving there are seventeen of us. We have been so blessed.

The letters you've just read from Richard and Roland Marshall give witness to the power of faith, love and hope. Their lives are an example of what can be accomplished when there is respect and caring within a family. I began this book with a simple poem. I am closing the book with a poem that has been a favorite of mine for many years. As I read it I am reminded of the many wonderful people who are a part of this book. Not just the ones quoted but also their parents and all who have influenced them during their lives. In a very real sense they have all been bridgebuilders. It is my hope that their words and mine will help make the crossing easier for the next generation of twins.

The Bridge Builder

An old man going a lone highway
Came at the evening, cold and gray,
To a chasm vast and wide and steep,
With waters rolling cold and deep,
The old man crossed in twilight dim,
The sullen stream had no fears for him;
But he turned when safe on the other side,
And built a bridge to span the tide.

"Old man," said a fellow pilgrim near,
"You are wasting your strength with building here.
Your journey will end with the ending day,
You never again will pass this way.
You've crossed the chasm, deep and wide.
Why build you this bridge at eventide?"

The builder lifted his old gray head.
"Good friend, in the path I have come,"
He said, "There followeth after me today
A youth whose feet must pass this way.
The chasm that was as naught to me
To that fair-haired youth may a pitfall be;
He, too, must cross in the twilight dim—
Good friend, I am building this bridge for him."

by Will Allen Dromgoole

Epilogue

Twins have spoken. You have heard words from the hearts of twins from all walks of life. You have been able to get into the heads of happy twins, sad twins, frustrated twins, twinless twins and twins who are still working at understanding the relationship they have with their twin.

Had it not been for the willingness of these twins to explore their feelings this book would not, could not, have been written.

For two reasons I did not attempt to assess what it was in the relationship that made or did not make the twinship experience a happy one. First, I do not feel qualified to second-guess what another person is feeling—only that person really knows. I felt it not fair for me to risk being judgmental in evaluating what I felt was an excellent, a good or a fractured relationship. Secondly, I felt it would not be fair to the twins who so graciously agreed to be a part of my research. I have presented their remembrances and feelings about their twinship as best I knew how. To the reader it may appear there was a lack of consistency and format as I presented the various twin sets. However, as I poured over the questionnaires of more than 800 identical and fraternal twins, I soon became aware that each twin set was unique (as it should be) and that each of the twins in every set was expressing his own feelings, apart from his twin. This was a very difficult task for some twins. Twins expressed themselves more fully in some areas than in others. Some of them were more comfortable talking about their childhood experiences, others appeared to avoid exploring their feelings about the parent/child relationship, etc. In some instances there was total avoidance in sharing their thoughts about their adult relationship.

As we all know, some people have the ability to express themselves on paper, some prefer to do it on a person-to-person/ eye-to-eye level. We know, too, that some of us can write on and on about our feelings, while others of us are more reserved and guarded in sharing thoughts. Often I was impressed at the number of men who appeared to welcome the opportunity to write their heretofore unexpressed feelings about twinship.

All of the people represented in the book gave permission to use their material. Most gave permission to use their names. In order to avoid any chance of identifying someone who chose not to be identified, I elected to use fictitious names for the twin sets with one exceptions.

These twin sets have made it possible for other twins to see the struggles for identity that some twins have known. They have shown how competition with their twin has kept some of them from exploring other avenues of interest in order to avoid competition with their twin.

Twins have given invaluable tips to parents of twins. They have told what it was they would like to have experienced in their developmental years—valuable tips for parents with little ones. Perhaps from their suggestions, parents of twins will be able to avoid some of the mistakes these adult twins knew as children.

Hopefully, those who have married a twin will learn the keys to successful twin marriages.

Family harmony is something all families want, but it does not always come easily or without work and concentrated effort. We have seen how the introduction of twins into a family can upset the proverbial 'apple cart.' I recall what one mother told me her little daughter said to her when she brought two babies home. She politely asked that one be sent back.

It is truly a huge adjustment for the entire family to make when two new little members join the already established family. It's worth all the effort parents of twins can muster to see that children are encouraged to build a bond with each of their siblings, older and younger. They will need to pull on that bond when parents are no longer around. The rewards of seeing them enjoy one another will be tremendous.

When I started researching twins, there was a scarcity of material focusing on the psychological impact of being a twin. I am happy to say great strides have been made the past ten years in educating people about twins. Twins themselves are now able to find material that will help them better understand themselves, their twin, and people's reactions toward them.

The quality of the relationship we have with others very often depends on how well we know ourselves. We relate better with others when we know 'who we are.' When we seriously work to find out what makes us do what we do, and act as we do, we are taking the first step in grasping just who we are. And how do we go about understanding ourselves? An easy question? Not at all. It is a difficult question but any effort at doing so will pay off with fantastic rewards and greater relationships with people.

In this whirling fast-paced world that seems to have all of us spinning most of the time, I fear it's the unusual person who says "Whoa! Wait a minute, give me time to catch my breath." I see the hurry flurry pace my grandchildren are sucked up into, (almost like a vacuum) and wonder what they will recall of their childhood except to remember the TV, the rush to activities, deadlines in school assignments, etc. Where can they go to find quietness, to sit and watch the clouds shift into different formations, to catch the early morning sounds from a farm, to see the close-up formation of a flower?

In closing, I feel I should address a question that may surface in the minds of some of my readers. "What about your relationship with your twin?" As I mentioned in my first book, one reason for my exploring twins was to help me in my own quest for a better understanding of my own twinship. It is a fair question and certainly one I am willing to share.

I do understand my own relationship with my twin better since having researched twins. Prior to my study I always felt since we were twins we should be more alike; share more time together and communicate on a deep emotional level. I have since learned that I, as a fraternal twin, share the same number of genes that any other siblings within a family share.

My twin sister and I were nurtured in the same environment, yet I'm sure we perceived our experiences differently. What I recall as a highlight of my childhood she might not remember. What might have been for her a memorable experience I might not recall.

Prior to my being held back in the fourth grade, due to illness, I recall always being together, sharing the same illness, sharing the same playmates and functioning as a team. As in most all twin sets there is a leader to some degree. My memory sees me as the less verbal and more passive twin (if true I must admit that I've made up for it over the years.) I thought of my twin as the more attractive, the smarter (probably due in part to my flunking the fourth grade, and the more aggressive. It didn't help my self-image when the comment would come from people, "You two don't look like twins," and "What grade are you girls in?" I regret that their questions had such an impact upon me as a child.

My twin sister and I share many traits, but we are different, too. And that is as it should be. We have both been blessed with lovely families and have been able to serve our communities and people in a helping capacity in diverse ways. I've observed this is natural for most twins since they have been born with a built-in companion and playmate—another with whom they have shared their time, thoughts and toys all their growing up years.

I've observed the intense togetherness and closeness of some identical twins and thought how wonderful that must be. My twin and I do not have to be with each other on a daily or weekly basis. We each feel secure in knowing the activities of one another. Since we live in the same city we talk briefly most every day, but do not see one another on a weekly basis. Yet, I cherish the special times when we do have lunch or go shopping together. During these times I feel a bit of the gaiety and carefree state I felt when we were small. In fact we've been surprised a few times when we'd both start to express the same thought. I believe our childhood of togetherness has left it's mark on both of us. We have much love and respect for one another. I will be forever thankful for the gift of my twin sister who in many ways watched over me as we were growing up. Her early acceptance of that role has stood her in great stead for the many times she has been asked to assume that role as an adult. I love her dearly and I know she loves me too. Of this both of us are confident: We have and always will be there for one another—*what security* that is for both of us.

Suggested Reading

Twins: Nature's Amazing Mystery, Kay Cassill.
Anthenum, 1982.

The Curious World of Twins, Margaret and Vincent
Gaddis. Hawthorn Books, Inc. *(no longer in print–
check libraries)*

*The Joy of Twins: Having, Raising and Loving Babies
Who Arrive in Groups.* Pamela Patrick Novotny.
Crown, 1988, Publishers, Inc.

*Having Twins, a Parent's Guide to Pregnancy, Birth and
Early Childhood.* Elizabeth Noble. Houghton
Mifflin, 1980, revised edition 1991.

*Make Room for Twins, a Complete Guide to Pregnancy,
Delivery and the Early Years.* Terry Pink Alexander.
Bantam Books, 1987.

Twins: An Uncanny Relationship, Peter Watson. Viking,
1981.

Identity and Intimacy in Twins. Barbara Schave and Janet
Ciriello, Greenwood Press, 1983.

Psychology of Twinship, Ricardo C. Ainslie, University of Nebraska Press, 1985.

The Care of Twin Children: A Common Sense Guide for Parents, Rosemary T. Thoreaux and Josephine F. Tingley, Center for Study of Multiple Gestation, Suite 464, 333 Superior Street, Chicago, IL 60611.

Twins and Supertwins, Amram Scheinfeld. Baltimore, Penguin, 1973. *(no longer in print–check libraries)*

Twins: Twice the Trouble, Twice the Fun, Philadelphia, Lippincott, 1965. *(no longer in print–check libraries)*

Struggling for Wholeness, Ann Kiemel Anderson and Jan Kiemel Ream. Oliver Nelson Books, a division of Thomas Nelson, Inc., Publishers, 1986.

Gemini: The Psychology and Phenomena of Twins, Judy W. Hagedorn and Janet W. Kizziar. Droke House/ Hallux, 1983. To place orders write or call: The Center for Study of Multiple Birth. 333 E. Superior St., Suite 464, Chicago, IL 60611, (312) 266-9093.

The Psychology of Twins, Herbert L. Collier, Ph.D. Books, Box N, 4227 North 32nd St., Phoenix, AZ 85018, 1974.

Twins on Twins, (photographs) by Kathryn McLaughlin Abbe and Frances McLaughlin Gill, Crown Publishers, New York, NY, 1980. *(no longer in print–check libraries)*

All About Twins, Dr. Gillian Leigh. Routledge and Kegan Paul, Great Britain, 1983.

Twins from Conception to Five Years, by Averil Clegg and Ann Woolett. Van Nostrand Reinhold Co., Inc., New York, NY, 1983.

My Twin and I, Ethel M. Jones. Carlton Press, Inc., 1987.

The Silent Twins, Marjorie Wallace. Prentice Hall, 1986.

The Twins Who Found Each Other. Bard Lindeman, William Morrow & Co., Inc., 1969.

Mothering Twins. Albi, Johnson, Catlin, Deurloo, and Greatwood. A Fireside Book, Simon & Schuster, 1993.

RESOURCES

International Twins Association, Inc.
Co-Secretary/Treasurers
Lynn Long and Lori Stewart
6898 Channel Road NE
Minneapolis, MN 55432
(612) 571-3022 or (512) 571-8910

The Twins Foundation
Kay Cassill, President
P.O. Box 6043
Providence, RI 02940-6043
(401) 274-8946
A Quarterly Newsletter, *The Twins Letter*

The National Organization of Mothers of Twins Clubs, Inc.
(NOMOTC)
P.O. Box 23188
Albuquerque, NM 87192-1188
(505) 275-0955

Lois Gallmeyer, Executive Secretary
Quarterly newsletter, *MOTC's Notebook*
Current membership as of February 1995: 20,500
Number of clubs as of July 1996: 470. Grandmothers,
legal guardians of multiples and godmothers are eligible to join.

The Center For Study of Multiple Birth
333 E. Superior St., Suite 464
Chicago, IL 60611
Dr. Louis G. Keith and Donald Keith, Co-directors
To place orders write or call (312) 266-9093

International Society For Twin Studies
c/o The Mendel Institute
Piazza Galeno, 500161
Rome, Italy
Publishers Acta Geneticae Medicae et Gemellologiae.
For more information contact:
Adam P. Matheny, Jr.,
c/o The Louisville Twin Study,
Child Development Unit,
2301 S. 3rd St.
Louisville, KY 40208
email: apmath01@ulkyvm.louisville.edu.

Parents of Multiple Births Association of Canada (POMBA)
240 Graff Avenue, Box 22005
Stratford, Ontario, Canada N5A 7V6, (519) 272-1926
email: pomba@cyg.net
Quarterly newsletter: *Double Feature*

***Twins* magazine**
5350 South Roslyn Street
Suite 400
Englewood, CO 80111
(303) 290-8500

Twin Services
P.O. Box 10066
Berkely, CA 94709
(510) 524-0863

The Triplet Connection
P.O. Box 99571
Stockton, CA 95209
(209) 474-0885
email: triplets@inreach.com
Double Talk
P.O. Box 412
Amelia, OH 45102
(513) 753-7117
Quarterly newsletter

Center for Loss In Multiple Birth, Inc. (CLIMB)
in care of Jean Kollantai
P.O. Box 1064
Palmer, AK 99645
(907) 746-6123

Mothers of Supertwins (MOST)
P.O. Box 951
Brentwood, NY 11717
(516) 434-MOST
email: mostmom@nyc.pipeline.com

Twinless Twins International
founder, Dr. Raymond W. Brandt (editor and publisher of
Twins World magazine)
11220 St. Joe Road
Ft. Wayne, IN 46835
(219) 627-5414
email: brandt@serv2.fwi.com

Darcie D. Sims
Psychotherapist and Grief Management Specialist
Contact Accord After Care Services
1941 Bishop Lane
Suite 202
Louisville, KY 40218
1-800-346-3087

The Twin to Twin Transfusion Syndrome (TTTS), Inc.
Mary Flaman-Forsythe, executive director
411 Long Beach Parkway
Bay Village, OH 44140
(216) 899-8887
email: tttsfound@aol.com

The Annual Twins Days Festival
P.O. Box 29
Twinsburg, OH 44807
(216) 425-3652

Organizations Abroad

South Africa Multiple Birth Association (SAMBA)
in care of Alida Vaneeden
Postbus 85445
Emmarentia 2029
Republic of South Africa

Twins and Multiple Births Association (TAMBA)
20 Redcar Close
Lillington
Leamington Spa. Warwickshire CV32 7SU
England

Australian Multiple Birth Association, Inc. (AMBA)
c/o The National Secretary
P.O. Box 105
Coogee, NSW 2034
Australia
(049) 46 8030

Multiple Births Foundation
Queen Charlotte's and Chelsea Hospital
Goldhawk Road
London, England W6OXG
(081) 748-4666 ext. 5201
email: mbf@rpms.ac.uk

New Zealand Multiple Birth Association
P.O. Box 1258
Wellington
New Zealand

Twin Research Study Questionnaire

Date_____

Identical: ☐ Boy/Boy ☐ Girl/Girl
Fraternal: ☐ Boy/Boy ☐ Girl/Girl ☐ Boy/Girl

Name: _____
        Last   First   Middle

Age: _____ Sex_____

Address: _____
          Street   City   State   Zip

Telephone: _____
            Home   Work

Name of Twin: _____
               Last   First   Middle

Address of Twin: _____
                 Street   City   State   Zip

Other Siblings: Older: ☐ Brothers ☐ Sisters
Younger: ☐ Brothers ☐ Sisters

Your schooling   Grade School

                        High School

                        College

                        Degree

Employment (title or position) _____

Other multiple births in family background?   ☐ Yes ☐ No

1. Were you the firstborn of the twins?   ☐ Yes ☐ No
2. Did you attend nursery school?   ☐ Yes ☐ No
3. Did you grow up in the same family?   ☐ Yes ☐ No
4. Did you grow up in a two-parent family?   ☐ Yes ☐ No
5. Do you feel that your childhood was
   generally emotionally secure?   ☐ Yes ☐ No
6. Did you attend the same school?   ☐ Yes ☐ No
7. Were you in the same classroom?   ☐ Yes ☐ No

8. If you were in the same classroom but later separated, at what grade level did this occur? _____

9. Did you share a lot of the same playmates? ☐ Yes ☐ No

10. Do you recall being dressed alike as small children ☐ Yes ☐ No

11. When older, did you choose to dress alike? ☐ Yes ☐ No

12. Were you usually given similar toys, gifts, etc. ☐ Yes ☐ No

13. Were birthdays ever celebrated on separate days? ☐ Yes ☐ No

14. As a child, were you often jealous of your twin? ☐ Yes ☐ No

15. As children, did you often consider yourself the leader? ☐ Yes ☐ No

16. While growing up, did you usually feel that you were in competition with your twin? ☐ Yes ☐ No

17. Did you usually feel that you were not as smart as your twin? ☐ Yes ☐ No

18. As children, were you often mistaken for one another? ☐ Yes ☐ No

19. Did you usually feel inferior to your twin? ☐ Yes ☐ No

20. Did you usually think of yourself as being less attractive than you twin? ☐ Yes ☐ No

21. Did you usually feel that you and your twin were being compared by family members and friends? ☐ Yes ☐ No

What were your feeling about this?

Please discuss.

22. As children, did you often feel dominated by your twin? ☐ Yes ☐ No

23. As children, did you share the same bedroom? ☐ Yes ☐ No

24. Did you share the same bed? ☐ Yes ☐ No

25. As you look back upon your childhood, is there anything that stands out as being very positive or negative as a result of your being a twin? Please discuss.

Parent / Child Relationship

1. Do you feel that your parents showed favoritism toward you? ☐ Yes ☐ No

2. Do you feel that your parents showed favoritism toward your twin? ☐ Yes ☐ No

3. Do you feel that your parents often compared your performance against that of your twin? ☐ Yes ☐ No

4. Were you ever given a derogatory nickname by either parent? ☐ Yes ☐ No

5. Do you feel that punishment was administered fairly by your parents? ☐ Yes ☐ No

6. Did your parents encourage you to develop your own extra-curricular activities? ☐ Yes ☐ No

7. If there is any aspect of your parent/child relationship which you would like to share, please do so.

Adult Relationship

Age_____

1. Do you usually enjoy being with your twin? ☐ Yes ☐ No

2. Has your feeling of closeness to your twin become greater as you have grown older? ☐ Yes ☐ No

3. At this stage of your life, do you have any feelings of competitiveness toward your twin? ☐ Yes ☐ No

4. Do you think you know your twin well? (Likes/dislikes?) ☐ Yes ☐ No

5. If you and your twin have children, have you ever felt that you compared the performances of your children? ☐ Yes ☐ No

6. Do you feel that you have a closer relationship with your twin than with other siblings, if any in family? ☐ Yes ☐ No

7. Have you ever given much thought to your twinship and the effects it may have had upon your life? Please discuss.

8. Do you believe that being a twin has had a definite effect upon your personality? Please discuss.

9. Do you feel that you are a more fulfilled or a less fulfilled person for having been a twin?

10. What would be the most important advice you could give to parents rearing twins?

11. Are there any interesting experiences in your own life, as a twin, that you would like to share?

12. How do you think society can help twins develop their individuality?

13. If we feel that your comments would be of special interest and/or help to others, would you give consent to their being published (without using your name)? ☐ Yes ☐ No

14. If additional information is needed, would you be willing to participate in a follow-up questionnaire? ☐ Yes ☐ No

Order Blank

I would like to order _____ copies of
Exploring Twin Relationships
USA: $14.95. Canada: $16.95. $3.00 S&H.

I would like to order _____ copies of
Living Without Your Twin
USA: $9.95. Canada: $11.95. $3.00 S&H.

I would like to order _____ copies of
We Are Twins But Who Am I
USA: $18.95. Canada: $21.95. $3.00 S&H.

Please send to:

Signature _____

Name _____

Address _____

City _____

State_____Zip _____

Send check or money order to:
Tibbutt Publishing
0438 SW Palatine Hill Rd.
Portland, OR 97219

Telephone orders 1-800-621-5655 or 1-800-356-9315 using
Visa, Mastercard or Discover.

ISBN 09629948-2-0